Punching Bag

Punching Bag

REX OGLE

Norton Young Readers

*An Imprint of W. W. Norton & Company
Independent Publishers Since 1923*

Copyright © 2021 by Rex Ogle

All rights reserved
Printed in the United States of America
First Edition

For information about permission to reproduce selections from this book, write to Permissions, W. W. Norton & Company, Inc., 500 Fifth Avenue, New York, NY 10110

For information about special discounts for bulk purchases, please contact W. W. Norton Special Sales at specialsales@wwnorton.com or 800-233-4830

Manufacturing by Lake Book Manufacturing
Production manager: Julia Druskin

ISBN 978-1-324-01623-6

W. W. Norton & Company, Inc., 500 Fifth Avenue, New York, N.Y. 10110
www.wwnorton.com

W. W. Norton & Company Ltd., 15 Carlisle Street, London W1D 3BS

2 4 6 8 0 9 7 5 3 1

To anyone who's ever been pushed down,
and needs a reminder to get back up—to stand again,
and keep reaching.

& for Marisa,
who never had a chance . . .
but has never let me give up on life.

AUTHOR'S NOTE

This is a true story. This is my story. It happened to me.

And as painful as it was for me to write, it may be equally or more painful for you to read—especially if you've lived through something similar.

If you're not ready to read this, then don't. Please, go enjoy some sunshine, watch a funny movie, or buy yourself an ice cream. This book will be waiting for you when you are ready.

But know this: I lived this, I survived. You survived your past too, or you wouldn't be here reading this. We are both alive. We may have a few more scars than we'd like—inside or out—but we made it through. No matter how dark the past, or even the present, the sun will always come up tomorrow. There is hope.

This story (and that ice cream) are waiting . . . whenever you're ready.

Punching Bag

homecoming

*P*eople get off the plane. I wait in my seat, feet not touching the floor. I remember my stuff in the pocket on the seatback in front of me. I put them in my blue-and-red backpack one at a time—a Mad magazine, a coloring book, a yellow box of forty-eight Crayola crayons. I double-check my shirt for the gold pin the pilot gave me. It has two wings on either side, with a circle in the middle that says Delta.

Outside the plane window, the night is dark. Lights blink in the distance, but all the shadows up-close seem different.

As the last people shuffle off, the plane gets quiet. Lights flicker, and seat belts hang loose off the sides of chairs. Overhead compartments are empty. Trash is in the aisle. For a second, I think I'm the last person on the plane, that they forgot about me, like all the magazines that people left behind.

Then the stewardess appears with a warm smile. "You ready, Rex?"

Kelly's hand is soft. She wears a stiff blue jacket and skirt. Her black shoes have little shiny dragon scales. I wonder if they're from a real dragon. With blond hair and firetruck-colored lipstick, she looks like a famous *actress I saw in a movie one time, except with shorter hair. She's real pretty. And nice too.*

When Kelly asks how old I am, I say, "Seven."

"Wow. I fly with a lot of kids, but I've never met a seven-year-old as brave as you."

I shake my head. "I'm not brave."

"Sure you are. You didn't get scared or anything. Most little kids get really frightened flying all by themselves. But not you."

"I was a little scared. But only during take-off."

Kelly laughs. "Then you did a good job of hiding it."

We walk into the warm light of the airport. The halls are filled with the hum of people talking or eating or rushing by. I'm wearing my backpack in front of me, squeezing it with my free arm.

From the other side of the glass, Mom raises her hand. All this joy floods through me. Three months in Tennessee with my dad's parents was nice. We went fishing. Hung out in the woods a lot. Went to church and sang hymns. I met cousins I didn't know about. But it's the longest I've ever been away from my mom. I missed her.

But Mom isn't smiling. Her boyfriend, Sam, stands next to her. He isn't smiling either.

Everything inside me sinks, like I swallowed a bunch of rocks.

"Is that your mom?" Kelly asks.

I want to say no. To stay with Kelly. Maybe she could adopt me. We could fly all over. Or maybe we could just get back on the plane. Back to Tennessee to my grandma June and pa-pa Rex. He and I have the same name, so everyone called me Bubba all summer. I didn't like it at first—but it's better than the names Sam calls me when he drinks too much.

Looking down, I notice. Kelly's shoes don't have dragon scales. They're just plastic.

"Rex, is that your mom?" Kelly asks again.

I nod.

Kelly lets go of my hand and squats down in front of me. She smiles her pretty Hollywood smile. "It was nice flying with you, young man." Then she gives me a big hug. I hold on for a while. She smells like flowers. Squeezing me, she says, "You stay brave."

I feel like I might cry.

I don't understand why I love my mom so much, and at the same time, why she makes me so afraid.

My legs carry me through the security door, out into the waiting area. Sam kneels, onto one knee, and hugs me real hard. "W-w-welcome home, k-k-kid," he stutters. Sam takes my backpack and leads the way.

Mom doesn't bend down. She side-hugs me, pressing me into her hip bone. Her hand on the back of my neck is dry and ice-cold, even though it's summer. Mom says, "So how was it?"

"Good," I say.

"Good?" Mom says. "That's it? Just good?"

I'm not sure what she wants me to say, so I just say, "Yeah, it was good."

"Did you have fun with your father?" When she says "father," she spits. I can tell she wants me to say no.

"He was only there for a week. Mostly, I was just with my grandparents. It was nice."

"Are you glad to be home?" she asks.

I nod.

"Aren't you going to ask about me?" she snaps. "You've been gone three months. Don't you care?"

I ask, "How was your summer?"

"Pretty shitty. I'll tell you all about it."

Sam stops walking. To my mom, he says, "D-d-don't."

In the crowded terminal, Sam's bottom jaw quivers, his eyes well up. "D-d-don't t-t-tell him, L-l-luciana. H-h-he's just a k-k-kid."

"If I have to live with it, so does he," she practically yells. I shrink a little when people turn their heads toward us.

Mom snatches my hand, squeezing it as we walk. Her grip is so tight, my fingers ache. I don't say anything until I lose feeling. I pull my fingers free. Mom shouts, "Why won't you hold my hand? Didn't you miss me?!" I let her grab my hand again, even though it hurts.

Her grip tightens. My fingers cry out, like they might shatter into pieces, like a porcelain bowl. I try to get my hand back, but it's locked tight. I whisper, "You're hurting me."

"No, I'm not!" Mom shrieks. "Don't be a baby."

"You are. Let go. Please?"

The whites of her eyes are streaked with red. Like she hates me. She throws my hand away from her, like a baseball. "Fine! I didn't realize I was so horrible to be around!"

"I didn't say that," is all I can whisper. My fingers are printed with red-and-white marks. I rub them. Mom's arms are crossed, shielding her from the world. From me.

The cool indoors air conditioning is sucked away as we walk through the automatic doors, into the pressing Texas heat. Mom's mood shifts as we turn into the parking lot. She smiles, and with a little laugh asks, "Are you ready to meet your sister?"

Planes fall from above, the sky falls too, then the stars, the moon, crushing and burying me. Only, nothing is really falling; it just feels that way. 'Cause I don't understand what she's saying. I don't know anything about a sister. She didn't tell me. Nobody told me. "What sister?"

Like I'm stupid, Mom snaps, "Your baby sister."

I check around me. No baby carriage, no stroller, no bag with diapers, nothing. No baby. "Where?"

"There's our car," she says. Mom opens the passenger door, pushing the front seat forward so I can crawl into the rear of the Toyota hatchback.

"L-l-luciana—" Sam says again.

She shoots him an icy glare. Then slips into the passenger seat and closes the door. From under her seat, she pulls out a little pink photo album. Sam gets into the driver's seat and tries to take the book away. "St-st-stop."

She slaps his hands away.

"Don't you dare touch me!" she yells.

"D-don't . . ." He looks all wrong when the tear slides down his face. He's a giant. Over six feet tall, his body all big muscles. But not now. Somehow he seems smaller. Shrunk. Not strong anymore. Like he might break too. "L-l-luciana. Th-th-this is wr-wrong. . . ."

"He needs to see it," Mom hisses.

"See what?" I ask.

"I-I-I'm s-s-sorry, R-r-rex," Sam stutters. "I-I-I'm s-so so s-sorry." He gets out, slams the door. He walks away. Ten feet, twenty feet, thirty . . . He keeps walking until I can't see him anymore.

"Sit in the middle, so you can see," Mom instructs me. I do. I lean forward between the two gray seats.

Mom opens the photo album.

There are pictures of a tiny baby girl. Her skin is tan and pink, a full head of wispy black hair, as fine as spider webs. She's wrapped in a pink blanket with white trim. Her eyes are closed. Maybe she's sleeping.

"This is your sister—" Mom starts. Mom is smiling, but her eyes are hollowed out. All this spit fills up in her mouth, coating her lips as she tries to talk, and starts crying. "This is your sister. Her name is Marisa."

"Marisa," I say. My sister. This warm feeling fills me up. "Where is she?"

"Right here!" Mom chokes, shaking the book. "Look! Look at the pictures!"

I do. But there are only six pictures. They all look the same. Marisa, wrapped in the pink blanket, eyes closed. She doesn't move. Or laugh. Or cry. Or drink from a bottle. She just lies there. Again and again and again in six photos. Her tiny fingers curled up in a small fist beside her little nose.

Whatever Mom is feeling infects me—like a sickness—'cause now I feel sick too.

I want to cry and scream and throw up. I want to run. Get out of the car. Escape. Go after Sam. He'll tell me what's happening. But I don't see him. And even though I don't like him, for some reason, I'd rather be with him. Or with Kelly, back on the plane. Or back in Tennessee. I wanna be anywhere else . . . anywhere but here . . . with my mom.

"Why aren't you looking at her?!" Mom screams. Tears and spit and snot run down her cheeks, her chin. A moan comes out of Mom, like a ghost.

Even though I don't want to know, I ask, "Mom, where is she?" Asking makes me burst into tears.

"Don't you cry!" Mom snaps. "Don't you dare cry! You weren't here. You didn't have to go through what I did."

I don't understand.

She shrieks, "You weren't here. You left. You left me."

I reach for my mom, trying to hug her around the seat. She slaps at my hands, pushes me away from her, from the photo album. She wraps her arms around it, around her heart. She screams, "Don't touch me!"

She tugs at her own hair, kicks the dashboard, throws herself against the door, slapping the window, howling.

"Mommy?" I whisper, crying. I didn't know. "Please . . ."

Curled up in the front seat, she thrashes wildly, turning, kicking, slapping, shrieking. "NO! NO! NO!" she bellows over and over, moaning, "Noooooooooo, no, no, no."

Something hits my face, maybe a foot or a fist. I don't know. I fall back, pressing myself into the backseat, trying to hide, trying to disappear.

My mom screeches and bucks and flails for a long time. Until she stops. She takes a heavy breath that shakes in the middle. Then another.

After a while, I reach around the seat, slowly, carefully, not to scare her, to hug her. She doesn't move. She's still as stone. Like she saw the snake-head woman in my Greek myth book.

Mom doesn't hug me back. That's OK. I wipe the snot from her nose, the spit on her chin. Her shirt is drenched with sweat. I hold her for a long time. She doesn't notice. 'Cause there's some kinda invisible wall between us. I can feel it now.

She finally whispers. "Sam may have hit me, but you left." Her eyes find mine in the crooked rearview mirror when she adds, "Your sister is dead. And it's your fault."

roadkill

The world is gray. 'Cause of the fog, there's a bit of wet and cold on everything. You can't see more than fifty feet out. Out past the cow pastures, there's just more fog, more mist. I can't see the shadows, but I can feel them.

Mom is driving me to the high school. My little brother, Ford, is sleeping in the backseat. The radio is on, but I'm not listening. I'm looking outside.

The sky is gray. The clouds are gray. The slick asphalt of the highway is wet black, striped with wet yellow and wet white lines. I watch the solid line outside my window turn away and return again and again. Like it can't help it. Like it has to stay. I don't know why the line can't just go off and go somewhere else. Somewhere safe.

The line is interrupted by a smear of blood, a pile of flesh.

A dead armadillo.

Armadillos are these little creatures the size of a cat. I'm not sure if they're lizards or mammals or what, but they have this kinda shell. Though I guess armor doesn't protect anyone from an eighteen-wheeler. I always thought armadillos were ugly. Now I feel bad for ever thinking that. My gut gets this ache, like I'm the one crushed on the side of the road.

"What time does the bus drop you off after school?" Mom asks.

I shrug. I don't say anything 'cause I don't know. I'm thinking about all the animals on the side of Texas highways. They're alive one second, then *BAM!* I wonder if the truckers even care. When they hit them, do they stop, or just keep going? Do they say a prayer or anything? My eyes get all hot. I try to stop thinking about all the dead animals.

Mom's fingers pinch an inch of my left arm, twisting.

"Ow!" I squeal. "What the hell?"

She shouts, "I asked you a question!"

"What?!"

"What time does the bus drop you off?"

"I said I don't know!"

"You didn't say anything!" Her voice is shrill. When I woke up, I could see it in her eyes that she was in a mood. Her eyes darting around all quick, like she's looking for something to be mad at. Usually, it's me.

I say, "School's out at three. So three thirty, I guess."

"You guess?"

"I don't know, OK? It's my first day of high school!" I don't mean to, but I'm shouting. When she raises her voice, I raise mine too. When she shouts, I shout back. When she screams, I scream. Like it's a contest. But she always wins.

"I don't see why a bus can't take you to school in the mornings too," Mom hisses.

"Because," I say for the hundredth time, "I have a zero-hour class. That means I have to come early, an hour before anyone else. They're not going to have a bus pick me up, drop me off, then go back and pick everyone else up."

"Why do you even have to take an extra class?"

"I don't *have* to. I *want* to." And I do want to. I like history. But more, I like being outside my apartment. That way, I don't have to be around Mom or Sam.

Plus, my counselor says a zero-hour class looks good on my high school transcript. You know, for college. Even though I don't know if I can go. 'Cause I can't afford it.

Next to me, Mom is muttering under her breath. "Always have to be the little overachiever, thinking you're so much better than me, well, you're *not*—"

My mouth opens, ready to yell. Tell my mom to shut up, that she should be supportive, like a real mom. That it's not my fault she dropped out of college; that was her choice.

Then, as if I'm not alone, my sister is there. She's maybe five or six. Beautiful, dark hair, a glow about her. Gently, as if she weren't a ghost in my mind, Marisa holds a finger up to her lips. She says, *Shhh.*

Mom hisses, "Little punk, like the world owes you something, well it doesn't, keep glaring at me like that, I'll bust you right in the face—"

Marisa shakes her head. *Don't take the bait.*

So I don't say anything. Instead, I bite the inside of my cheek. Biting down 'til the teeth break skin and I taste metal. Blood.

Marisa says, *Say something kind.*

Through gritted teeth, I say, "Thank you for taking me to school."

Mom huffs. Her eyes narrow, watching me like I'm a viper. Like it's some kind of trick. Finally she snaps, "I have to bring your brother out here to pre-K anyways."

In the back, Ford is fast asleep in his car seat. He's five, and seems so big now. Seems like just yesterday I was changing his diapers and washing his paci. Sometimes I wanna strangle him, but mostly I'm proud of him.

A burning smell stings my nose 'cause Mom's riding the clutch so hard. I don't even know how to drive, but I know better. I roll down my window. Let the morning air inside. I like the cold on my face. I avoid my reflection in the side mirror.

Mom snaps, "Roll up the window, it's freezing!"

"It's Texas in September. It's never really freezing."

Her whole face hardens into a glare. Like one of those presidents' faces in the mountain, but real pissed-off.

One last powerful gust of wind blows around the car, pushing up Mom's cut-off sweat shorts. Her right thigh isn't light olive like her left thigh. It's muddied with vibrant colors: the deep purple of eggplant, dark red like canned cranberry, sunflower yellow. All of it together looks like that modern painter who does stuff on big canvases. Or like those big giant clouds swirling in outer space as big as galaxies. Anywhere else, the colors would be pretty. Beautiful even.

But it's not. 'Cause it's on my mom's body.

I've seen it a hundred times on her.

And on me.

It's not paint. It's not the cosmos. They're bruises. Evidence of another fight.

Mom pushes her shorts down. I expect fury. I expect her to be angry or mad. Instead, all her anger goes out the window, chasing the wind. Her eyes get wet, and the tears well up, getting bigger and bigger, forming these like spheres around her eyes. And I wait. Watching. Waiting for them to fall. But they don't.

I feel like I'm always waiting for something.

For my dad to send the child-support check so we can pay our phone bill. For bad news like someone's sick or dying or already dead. For jerks at school to make fun of my shoes, with their holes in them, or my clothes from the secondhand store. For store clerks to give me those looks like they don't trust me 'cause of our neighborhood. For police, who sometimes drive by, scanning for the guy in our complex who sells weed but instead watch me, 'cause I'm at the playground, watching my brother on the swings. Or for our place to get robbed, again, or for my stepdad to come home in a mood, 'cause he's already been drinking and he's ready to rumble. For Mom to get in her dark mood, the one where she looks at me like I'm out to get her, 'cause the whole world is always out to get her and she can't trust anyone, not even me.

I hate waiting.

But I'm always waiting.

'Cause something bad is just around the corner.

Usually, it's a fist.

moving

"Rex, run back inside and make sure we didn't forget anything," Mom says.

I say, "We didn't."

"Just *do it*." The edge of her voice is sharp as a knife.

Mom goes back to arguing with Sam about who's gonna drive to our new place. If I were old enough to drive, I'd take my brother and drive away. I'd never look back.

Walking up to the old apartment, I freeze on the last stair. I always do that. It's like this step where I take a sec to catch my breath. Before I go inside. Before I face Mom and Sam and whatever mood they're in.

The breezeway is all gray peeling paint, spider webs, the smell of must and mold. The area feels tight, claustrophobic. Like a dark cave leading to a darker place. I never liked it here.

Stepping inside, I realize it's for the last time. Two years here. Now it's empty, like a place from a dream, like I know it, but I don't. But I do know it. All of it. I can't forget.

In the living room, there's a crater where you can see the apartment's insides, drywall and wood beams. Folks who came over always asked, "Is that a rug on the wall?" They didn't know it covered up a hole the size of my mom's body, from where she'd been thrown into the wall like an asteroid into the moon.

The kitchen cabinets are bare except an army of ants searching for leftovers. Pressed into the dining area carpet is a big "X" from the table. Tiny bits of broken brown and emerald glass are tucked, hidden away in the corners and carpet seams. When they catch the light just-so, they remind me of pirate jewels instead of shards from broken beer bottles.

The hall is empty, but it was always empty. Except for four scratches on either side, from when Mom clawed to stop herself as Sam dragged her by one leg into their bedroom, to continue a fight behind a closed door.

We all shared one bathroom. It's empty now, except stray hairs and soap crud.

Mom and Sam's bedroom is empty, too, as though no soul ever slept there.

My bedroom shows no signs of furniture, because I didn't have any. My sleeping bag was in the corner. But I trace my fingers along the walls over hundreds of tiny pockmarks, from where I tacked up sheets to make forts for me and Ford to hide in, as if linens and fantasy could protect us.

Two years we called this space home. Tomorrow, the maintenance man will come to patch the holes and tighten the pipes. Cleaners will clean the carpet, and a maid will scrub out the stains left behind on the linoleum floors. Painters will roll over the wall with a wet coat of fresh white. Then next week, a new family will move in to make new memories.

I desperately hope that their memories of this place will be better than mine.

new place

"Morrigan Place is going to be nicer than anywhere we've ever lived," Mom says. Her face wears a big smile like she won the lottery. "It has two pools, a playground for Ford, a fitness center—"

"You've never been to a gym in your life," I say.

Mom laughs. "Maybe I'll start!" She moves her arms like she's on an elliptical. Ford does too.

"The complex is only a few years old, so everything is brand-spanking-new."

I'm trying not to get my hopes up.

But when our borrowed truck pulls up, my face presses to the window. The colors are a little weird, with crimson brick and turquoise-painted wood. Mom is right though, everything looks new. It is nice. The grass doesn't have big brown patches and trash scattered around like the last few places. A tall fence surrounds the whole complex, including the parking lot. You need a special code to get inside.

I ask, "Is it government-subsidized?"

Mom rolls her eyes. "No. Sam and I are both working now. We can pay the rent on our own, thank you very much."

"What's the rent?"

"N-n-none of y-your b-bees-wax," Sam stutters.

I get real annoyed. Every month, it's me who balances the checkbook to make sure Mom doesn't overdraft the account. When they decided to move, Mom and Sam didn't even talk to me. They make a little over a thousand dollars together, which seems like a lot. But after bills, there's nothing left. If the rent is more than six hundred a month, we're gonna be in trouble.

"Here's our place!" Mom says.

"We're next to the pool?" Ford asks.

"Yup. Barely twenty feet away," Mom says.

The building is clean. The second-floor patio looks over the pool, the parking lot, and the lot across the street that's all grass and a few cattle.

"I bet the view up there is nice," I say. "I can do my homework in the sun."

"W-we're not on the s-second floor," Sam growls.

I look at Mom. "You told me it was on the second floor. That you would never live on the first floor, because you can always hear the upstairs neighbors."

Mom avoids eye contact with me. "They wanted a hundred more for upstairs. Stupid, right? Downstairs is the same size though. Two bedroom, one bath."

Sam shoves a box into my arms. "M-make y-yourself useful."

Inside, Mom points out my room. It's the darkest in the apartment. It faces the patio, which sucks, 'cause there's a big cross-hatched fence blocking any view. It makes the room feel like a cage. I open the window to let in fresh air. This is my new room. My new life. I need to get used to it.

"*Ándale*, w-wetback," Sam says. "L-let's g-go!"

"Don't call me a wetback," I say.

"OK, b-beaner." Sam laughs.

Ford laughs too. For some reason that makes me more mad. Not at my little brother. At Sam. If he hates Mexicans so much, why is he with my mom?

And why is she with him?

But that's the question I'm always asking.

Every. Single. Day.

It takes less than an hour to bring in our stuff. We don't have a lot. Couch, TV console, velvet recliner, and Mom's bed: that's all the furniture. Then the TV, the toaster, a few boxes of kitchen stuff, Ford's toys, and some other junk. All my books fit in two shoeboxes. The rest is just clothes in garbage bags. My folks' work uniforms are on wire hangers pushing through a trash bag. When Sam tosses it to me, my arms get clawed. I scream and drop it.

The bag looks like a porcupine, little hooks stabbing out of the thin black plastic like quills. My forearms are all cut up and bleeding, like a cat got me.

"D-don't b-be such a b-baby," Sam says.

"Yeah," Ford says, "baby."

We stick our tongues out at each other.

Ford blocks the doorway to our bedroom, shouting, "This is my room! All mine!"

"Not even," I say. "We have to share."

"Nuh-uh!" Ford shouts. He kicks me in the shin.

Sam laughs. "T-t-tell 'em who's b-b-boss, Ford."

I shove past Ford into our room. I unroll the sleeping bag, unzip it so it lies open, to see how much space we have left. This room is smaller than our last, but has a ceiling fan. I put Ford's pillow and blanket on his side (closer to the door), then my pillow and blanket on my side (by the window). Ford's toys go in one corner, my books in the other. After laying down some trash bags on the closet floor, I refold our shirts and shorts and socks, one at a time, then place them inside. A lot of my friends have messy rooms. They toss their stuff around wherever. Maybe 'cause they have so much stuff.

"Let's go to La Casa for dinner," Mom says, "to celebrate our fresh start."

"Fresh tart?" Ford asks.

"Fresh *start*," Mom says. "We have a new home. A clean slate. We get to start over. Everything in the past is in the past."

"G-g-great idea." Sam leans over and takes Mom's hand. They kiss.

For a second, for the fastest of moments, I have this flash in my head. Of Mom and Sam always being like this, all sweet to each other. Happy, smiling. And me and Ford, and even my sister. She's beside me, a year older than Ford. She'd have her own pink sleeping bag on the other side of the room. But she wouldn't laugh at Sam's jokes about me being part Mexican. 'Cause she's not like that. She's better.

But all of that's in my head. When I remember it's not real, this pit in my stomach opens up. Like there's something missing inside me. Or, like the past isn't in the past. It's still here, a ghost hanging over us.

Sam whispers something into Mom's ear. She giggles. Mom

says, "You two should go explore the playground or something." Then they disappear inside their bedroom and close the door.

A shadow settles over me like winter. Not a real shadow, not anything you can see. 'Cause the sun is out and the sky is blue and it's warm for everyone else but me. I don't know why no one else can feel it but me, but everything is in this gloom. Like it's eating us.

I go about my day and stuff, but I'm only half there. Even with me and Ford walking around, checking out the lay of the land, even with me pushing him on the swings, even when I meet some neighbor kids who are nice. I mean, I'm laughing and doing stuff, but I'm not there, not all of me. 'Cause half of me is in that dark place, waiting for things to get worse.

It lasts all day. When we get to my favorite restaurant, La Casa, the lights even feel darker. I ask the waitress if the lights are dimmed, but she gives me a weird look and says no, there's only one setting. Even with chips and salsa and queso, and their little mini-tacos that I always get, even with the year-round Christmas lights hanging overhead, and the mariachi band playing—I can't shake it, all this darkness welling up inside.

I want a fresh start. I really do. More than anyone.

But I don't know if I can start again, not until my mom leaves Sam.

And she won't.

Sleeping, I dream of battling alongside the X-Men against an alien race called the Brood. I have superpowers, and I'm fighting to save the world. Even though it's supposed to be scary, I'm not scared. 'Cause I have powers and I'm fighting monsters. I'm not helpless.

But the dream fades, and the screams become real.

At first I don't know where I'm at. The door and the window are all wrong. This isn't my room. It takes me a minute to wake up, to remember we moved. Ford is curled up next to me. The clock says it's almost two in the morning.

Mom and Sam are shouting in the living room. There's a loud thud. A body slamming into a wall, followed by a wail. Mom's.

My heart starts to slam against my chest. Ford opens his eyes, looks at me. His eyes glisten in the dark.

I say, "*Shhh.* Go back to sleep."

"Leave me alone, you bastard!" Mom shouts. This building might be new, but the walls are thin. "Help! Somebody help me!"

In the darkness, I fumble for my backpack. I take the U2 mix tape out of my Walkman, and slip in a storybook cassette, the one I got from the library. I put the headphones over Ford's ears and press Play.

Mother Goose reads rhymes to Ford, but he's still looking at me. Gently, I lay him back down, wrap him in my blanket, and give him my stuffed penguin, the one I never let him play with 'cause my aunt Lora got it for me. I tack the sheet four feet up the wall, then into the windowsill on the next wall, making a tent. The quilt Abuela made for us I make into a door. Ford is tucked away, safe. But not really.

In the next room, Mom is crying. Sam is yelling. My breathing skips an inhale. I sit in the dark, outside the tent, guarding. I don't let their fights come to Ford. He's too young. He doesn't understand.

"Stupid b-bitch!" I don't need to see Sam to know he's drunk. I hear it in his voice. Three margaritas at dinner, the twelve-pack he picked up on our way home.

"Stay away from me! Don't touch me! I'll leave you! I mean it this time. I'll take the boys. I'll go to my mother's!"

Sam laughs. He knows she won't.

I hear hand slapping flesh. Hers or his, I don't know. Something crashes into the wall. Shatters.

My back is against the door now. Wrapping my arms around my knees, I make myself a boulder. They can't get in if I sit here. Ford will be safe.

A body hits the floor. Mom is screaming, "Let go!"

Every muscle in my body tenses so hard I can't move. My throat closes, so I can't breathe. What do I do? Run away with Ford? To where? Go out there, try to help my mom? I've tried. It never works. It makes it worse. Sam is twice my size. He ends up beating me too. Then the next day, they're both mad at me.

Why won't she just leave him?

I stand up.

The air is cold 'cause my body is soaked with sweat. But I'm hot at the same time. I'm aware, but not, of wearing nothing but thin plaid boxers.

I go to the door. My hand is on the knob, but it refuses to turn. Like some part of me wants to stay safe, here on this side of the door. Let them finish. Maybe they're almost done.

Mom's crying turns into a wail.

Usually she screams and punches back. Her war cries let me know she's OK. I know she's not hurt too bad if she can insult him. Call him names. Tell him he's worthless.

But she's not doing that. She's just sobbing.

My mind is all images of what's on the other side of the door, all things I've seen before . . . Her on the ground, him on top, his fist rising and dropping, or holding her down, his elbow crushing her head into the ground as he shouts how crazy she is . . .

I wonder if she's bleeding. If he's knocked out a tooth. If her bones are broken.

My hand won't turn the knob. I'm too scared.

And then I'm thinking about her again. My sister, I mean. The airport, Sam crying, Mom and those horrible photos. The memory is burned into my brain. Like a scar.

I still wonder, what happened that night. I wasn't there, but I've tried to put together the pieces. The same as usual? Sam drinks. Mom yells. They start fighting. Then Mom, swollen belly, pregnant with my sister, is shouting in his face. Sam swings.

And Marisa never draws a breath.

She never even gets the chance.

Why is Mom with him? Why did she stay? Eating meals with him, laughing with him? A year later, they had Ford, which I can't even understand, and it makes me want to scream and cry and fight the world.

And my sister whispers in my ear, *Breathe.*

My lips and lungs quiver at the inhale.

Listening at my bedroom door, I hear a tiny gasp. And another. Like Mom is wheezing, like she can't breathe . . .

I hear her voice, tiny and far away, weak and scared . . . "Rex—"

I stop thinking and open the door.

A clump of Mom's thin brown hair lies on the carpet. Not far from the shards of the broken lamp. And Sam, his huge frame hovering over my mom, his knee pressed into her neck. Her face is bright crimson, starving for air.

I throw myself at Sam. I shove over and up, pushing with everything I have. He's like a wall. Me against a mountain. He doesn't move.

He calls me "s-sissy" and bats me away. I'm up, behind him, grabbing his face. One finger catches a nostril, another his mouth. For the rest, I dig in with my nails. When he pushes me away again, I take skin with me. He roars. I lunge and shove again, pushing him over.

Mom flies across the room like a wind-up mouse. She makes it to the far corner in the dining room, slamming into the wall. I'm watching her, watching me. Then Sam's fist hits my chest like a sledgehammer. The air rushes out, punched out of my lungs, like the time I fell off a jungle gym in fifth grade.

On the ground, I writhe. My body doesn't listen when my brain tells it to run. I jerk and spasm, clutch at the carpet, trying to get air into my lungs.

Sam's hand touches his face. His fingers spotted with blood. "Y-you sc-scratched me, l-little f-faggot!" He stands. He kicks me in the stomach. "G-get up and f-fight like a m-man."

My body aches, desperate for air. My fingers at my throat, pulling at it, trying to coax in just one little gasp of air. Tears rush down my cheeks. I wonder if my lungs are broken, if I'm going to suffocate, if I'm going to die.

"G-g-get up." Sam's stutters turn into shouts. "G-g-get up!"

I don't.

I can't.

And even if I could—

I am rocking on the ground, grasping my chest, my insides on fire. Starving for the smallest breath. The pain takes over every inch. And I find myself staring at the ceiling, at the strange spackled paint treatment. Like upside-down snowy mountains. Like I'm floating above myself. Drifting.

Like I've left my body.

The pain is gone. The hurt is calm. The burning in my lungs feels far away.

And I worry: Am I dying? 'Cause I won't get into heaven. 'Cause I'm not a good person. 'Cause I have terrible, evil thoughts, all the time. 'Cause I left my mom when she needed me most. 'Cause it's my fault my sister died.

Sam is about to kick my body again, when Mom leaps onto his back. "*Leave him alone!*" Her fists pummel him, hit him, she pulls at his neck. He spins, trying to throw her off. He loses his balance. They tumble onto the couch, roll off, land on the floor.

Then the pain comes rushing back as I return to my body. And air rushes into my lungs. Not all, but just enough to gasp and choke for another.

Mom and Sam tussle next to me but I can't focus on them. All I can do is roll onto my side, then onto my stomach. I push up, gripping the carpet, trying to help my body bend, open my airway so I can steal a full breath.

Flashing red and blue whirls off the blinds from outside.

For a split second, I think it's a carnival. I don't understand why they would set up here, outside our apartment. Then I hear car doors close. Two figures walk by, passing in front of the windows, jangling clinks sounding on their belts, a *clip-clop* of uniform boots. There's banging at the door.

"Police. Open up!"

Mom and Sam are outside with the two officers. Mom is shaking her head, no, no, no. Sam stands there, quiet, hands behind his back. A light turns on in a neighbor's window. They step forward to watch through their blinds as I watch through mine.

I unlock the window, push up, opening just an inch. So I can hear.

"—told you already, it's all a misunderstanding," Mom growls at the police. "Sometimes we argue. Every couple does. You can't throw us in jail for being normal!"

"Ma'am, we need you to calm down."

"We didn't do anything wrong! What I want to know is who called you? They don't know what's happening inside my home. Make them come out and face me. I'll tell it to their face!"

"That won't be necessary."

"Sir, have you been drinking?" One of the cops holds a flashlight in Sam's face.

"A-a l-l-little."

"Drinking isn't illegal!" Mom snaps. "He didn't drive. He was drinking at home."

"Ma'am, you seem agitated—"

"I am agitated!" Mom snaps. "You come here, banging on my door at two in the morning, waking me up—"

"You were sleeping?"

"No, but I was about to go to sleep!"

"Ma'am. Your shirt is torn. Your nose is bleeding. And you look like you've been crying. Is there anything you want to tell us?"

"No! Of course not!" Mom says, her voice twisting and rising midsentence. There's a long pause after.

In the headlights of the police car, Mom's face is all distorted. Her eyes wild, her toothy grin ripping across her face, and the shadows beneath her eyes darker than usual. She looks possessed. She starts laughing, but not happy laughing. "No, no. Everything's fine."

The whole thing makes me think of the Joker, Batman's worst enemy.

One of the cops waves Mom to the side, away from Sam. It's closer to me, so I hear better. "Ma'am, if you're too scared to say anything—because *he's* here"—the cop nods to Sam—"please know that you are safe with us here. We are here to protect."

I realize I'm holding my breath. Mom could stop this. She could fix this. She could make everything right.

Sam will go to jail.

He won't hit her again. He won't hit me again. And if he doesn't hit her, she won't hit me. All the hitting and the kicking and the slapping and the screaming, it'll all stop.

We'll be free.

Mom sees me in the window. Her eyes lock on mine.

In my head, I tell her, *Do it. Say he's guilty.*

Instead, she says, "I swear, on my mother's grave. Everything is fine."

I feel weightless. Like the ground falls away, like gravity forgets me. I sit there at the window, not understanding. Why doesn't she say something? Anything? Why not just tell the truth?

The officer's flashlight shines on my face. "Ma'am, is that your son?"

Sam says, "F-f-fuck."

"Ma'am, could you ask your son to come out here and join us please?"

Mom crosses her arms, like she's suddenly remembered to be cold. She walks to the apartment, slowly, so I can see her

glaring at me. When she opens the door, she says, "Come here."
Under her breath, she hisses, "Don't. Say. *Anything.*"

One officer stays with Sam. The other walks over to me.
"Are you OK?"

I nod.

"See? He's fine! It's a school night. Can he go to bed now?"

The officer looks at Mom with agitation.

"Ma'am, go stand over there with your boyfriend."

"No, this's my son, I'm not—"

The officer's face hardens, and Mom shuts up. She joins
Sam. They're both watching me, like owls watch mice. The cop
bends over slightly, so we're face-to-face.

"You can tell me if something's not right. If that man over
there is hurting you or your mother, you can say it."

I look at the cop's face, at his green unwavering eyes. At the
golden badge on his chest. Past him, Mom and Sam stare at me.
Sam's eyes look scared. Mom's are all fury, almost daring me to
do the wrong thing.

"Son?" the officer says again. His green eyes are warm,
accepting. He wants to help me. I wish he were my father.

Now I don't know what to say.

Tell the truth, or lie.

I want to tell the truth. Desperately.

I want to never see Sam again. My sister is dead because
of him.

But he's also Ford's dad. I don't want Ford to have to go to
prison to see him. What if Mom gets in trouble too? Would me
and Ford go into the foster system?

If they just take away Sam, can we afford rent? If Sam goes

and Mom stays, will she be pissed at me? She wants me to lie—
to keep lying. Would anyone believe me now?

The officer has a seven-pointed star patch on his shoulder.
It says "Birmingham Police," "State of Texas," and "*Sine cera.*" I
don't know what the last part means. It's another language, but
I don't know which one.

"Son, are you OK?"

"Yeah," I finally say. "I'm fine. Everything's fine."

laundry

When I get home from school, Nina Simone is singing in our living room. The vinyl record spins delicately on the player, circling again and again. Mom dances in her own circle with Ford, holding him in her arms. She spins, laughter rising out of her. She looks younger. Like a teenage girl. Not a mom. Not my mom. She twirls, swaying her hips, bending wrists just so. I wonder if this is what she was like before us. Carefree. Happy.

Then she sees me. She plops Ford onto the couch and approaches. Her hands find my shoulders as she looks into my eyes. Discomfort boils up in my gut. I step back.

"I'm not dancing with you. It's incest."

"Don't be stupid," Mom says. She tries to guide my hands to her hips, but it's too weird. I pull away.

"Ugh, never mind," she growls. She yanks the needle off the record player, sending a shrieking scratch through the speakers. For two long, tense seconds, I think she'll explode. But instead, she switches the record to Whitney Houston.

At the dining-room table, I start my homework. Even though we have a dishwasher, Mom washes the dishes by hand. She sings the whole time. That, with the sun outside and the windows open and the breeze coming in, everything feels almost normal. Like a TV show.

Mom is all over the apartment: dusting, picking up Ford's toys, folding blankets, vacuuming, fluffing couch cushions. Then she drops the laundry basket next to me. "There's a roll of quarters in my purse."

"I'm doing my homework."

Mom's icy glare doesn't care. I bookmark my place and close my textbook. When I go to pick up the basket, I stop. "What is *that?*"

"What is what?" Mom asks.

I'm pointing at Sam's Jockey briefs. They're white—except for a long brown stain.

"Is that—?"

Mom slaps me with a dish towel. She's actually trying not to laugh. "Just do the laundry."

"I am *not* washing his dirty underwear with my clothes. That's unsanitary."

"What is it?" Ford asks.

I point at the top of the laundry pile.

He stares for a minute. "Is it chocolate?"

"Something like that."

Ford leans over and sniffs. "That's poo!!"

Laughter bursts out of me, like a shotgun. I can't stop laughing.

"Who pooped their clothes?" Ford asks.

"The only one in this house who wears men's briefs," I say. "Your dad."

Ford's face goes crooked as he bares his teeth. "My dad?!"

Now we're both laughing.

I grab my homework pencil, using it to lift Sam's briefs away from the pile. Whispering to Ford, "Nope. I don't want his poo touching our clothes." Ford puts both hands over his mouth, cackling through his fingers. I dig through the basket, and discover four more pair of Sam's underwear. Two more of them are soiled.

"I'm gonna throw up," Ford says.

"Me too."

Mom says, "Grow up. Both of you. Rex, do the laundry."

But I see it in her face. Some part of her, trying not to smile—but failing. So I keep going. "Mom. Please tell me, how long has this been going on? How long have you been washing the excrement out of Sam's trousers?"

"It's *not* funny!" she says. "It's not a lot!"

I ask, "I mean, is this what true love is? Washing your partner's dirty deeds? Doesn't he know how to wipe?"

"Stop it!" Mom says. Her face is turning red.

"This matter is very serious," I say. "This is a very serious *fecal* matter."

"Rex, stop!" Tears come out of Mom's eyes as she bursts into laughter. Her smile is like the sun and the blue sky after a nuclear winter. My heart buoys up into my chest and it's almost hard to breathe. I don't want this moment to go away.

I ask, "Is there some kind of spray I should use first? Crap-Be-Gone?"

"It's not like he does it all the time!" Mom shouts, but lightly, and with a chuckle. It's a different kind of shout I've never heard. Joyous.

"Would you say *some* of the time, or *most* of it?"

"*I* don't even do that!" Ford says. "Daddy needs diapers."

"I'm with my brother! You know what, Mom. I'm happy to do the laundry, but only the non-manure clothes. When Sam gets home from work, he can wash these himself."

Sam's soiled garments are lying, stain-up, on his dining-room chair.

I'm on the couch doing my homework. Ford is watching cartoons. When either of us looks over, we snort and chortle.

Mom says, "You better move those before he gets home. You don't know what kinda mood he'll be in."

"I'll risk it," I say. "What's the worst he'll do? Smack me around? That'll happen eventually anyway, whatever I do."

"Rex," Mom says. This time, her words come out like a snare, warning me.

I shrug. Then smile. "Too late. I already threw out the pencil I used to move those there. I'm not touching them again. If you're worried, you move them."

She doesn't. The same devilish glint is in her eye.

She wants to poke the bear too.

When Sam opens the door, the acrid stench comes in first, chemical lawn fertilizer soaked into his uniform and skin. He kicks off his black rubber boots outside, then makes his way toward the bathroom. "H-h-hey, F-ford, R-rex."

We exchange a brotherly glance, smothering our snickers.

When Sam kisses Mom outside the bathroom, he asks, "Wh-what are y-ya'll sm-smiling 'bout?"

"Nothing," Mom says. After the bathroom door closes and the shower turns on, her hand covers her giggles.

Sam comes out wearing sweats and a T-shirt, smelling of Dove bar soap. He runs his hand through his hair, then stops. "Wh-what? Wh-why y-ya'll staring at m-me?"

Ford has no patience. He points at Sam's chair. "You poop yourself!"

Mom, me, and Ford all laugh.

I'm not sure what we expected, but Sam's reaction isn't it. He shrugs. "S-so?"

"So?" I ask. "So who does that?"

"They're just s-skid marks," he says.

"*Skid marks?* There's a name for it?"

"Y-yeah. Everyone h-has 'em."

"Um, no they don't," I say, pointing to all of the finished, folded, clean laundry on the dining-room table. "Feel free to inspect any of my underwear. They're skid-mark-free."

Sam shrugs again. "G-g-good for you."

"You need to learn how to wipe," Ford says.

"I w-wipe once. That's e-enough."

"Once? Once is not always enough. Sometimes you gotta do it twice. Or three or four times. Or more!"

"N-no, y-ya don't."

"Were you raised in a barn?" I shout.

Sam struts over, stands over me. "N-n-no." His chest bumps mine as he pushes past me. "G-growing up, e-each m-morning, my d-d-dad went in the b-b-bathroom and left f-four squares of toilet paper, one f-for each of my b-brothers and m-me. That's a-all we g-got."

"Are you serious?"

"As a r-r-rattlesnake."

"Why?"

Sam walks over and picks up his three pairs of briefs. He doesn't even wince when his thumb lands on a stain. "M-my folks g-grew up in the G-great D-depression. My dad m-made sure not to waste a s-single red cent. O-one s-square e-each."

"What if you needed more?" I ask.

"We d-didn't."

Then Sam tosses his underwear at me. Unfortunately, I don't duck in time.

crusts

"Where were you?!" Mom shouts, waiting at the apartment door, waitress apron in hand. She doesn't wait for an answer. She shoves past me.

"The school bus ran late," I call after her.

She flips me off.

Inside, Ford is sitting in the pink velvet chair watching cartoons. Not taking his eyes from the TV, he nods when I ask, "You want a snack?"

I shake a handful of Goldfish crackers into a paper bowl, then add two fingers of string cheese. "Scootch over," I say, shoving myself between him and the rest of the chair.

"No!" he whines, pushing with his arms, then trying to use his legs. I'm bigger though.

I could tell him to get up, make him sit on the floor, like his dad does me. But I don't. Instead, I let him get settled in my lap. I hold the bowl of crackers for him while he peels the cheese like a monkey does a banana.

Marisa comes to mind.

I wonder which cartoons she'd watch if she were here. If she and Ford would gang up on me when I try to sit in the chair. Would she eat the Goldfish like Ford, tossing them in her mouth and missing half the time? Or would she mummify the fish-shaped crackers in thin strands of string cheese like me? Nah. She'd be as stubborn as me and Mom. She'd have her own way of doing things. Maybe tying the mozzarella strings into bows around the Goldfish and saying a prayer before biting off their cracker tails.

I wonder, if my sister never died, would Mom be happy?

Maybe.

But I don't know.

After Mom goes to work, before Sam gets home, the apartment is all peaceful. Like a Texas town between tornados. Or a tomb, but in a good way, like an Egyptian one, with mummies and gold and adventures waiting for a hero.

After I finish my homework, I make sure Ford does his. We read for a bit, then I let him pick one of my toys to play with. On the top shelf of my closet, out of his reach, I have a few action figures: Star Wars, G.I. Joe, some Teenage Mutant Ninja Turtles. I know I'm too old for this stuff, but it still makes me smile inside, so I keep them even though I don't play with them.

The phone rings. Sam tells me he's grabbing drinks with Ray, that I don't have to worry about his dinner. I'm glad. Sometimes, he comes home in a shitty mood, and if dinner isn't waiting for him, still hot, he gets real pissy. It's better when he goes out.

I turn to Ford. "Looks like we're on our own tonight. What should we eat?"

Ford looks at me with his bowl haircut and big puppy-dog eyes. "Pizza?"

"I wish," I say. "We don't have money to order one. But I can make us something fun. Let's check the cabinets."

The two of us go in the kitchen. I think back to when our cabinets were always empty. But now, Mom and Sam can afford groceries. Though Mom still uses food stamps.

"Peanut butter jelly," Ford says.

"No cooking equals no cleaning," I say. "I'm down for PB&J."

Ford claps and does this funny little dance. He swings his hips and sings, "Peanut butter jelly! Peanut butter jelly!"

He's kinda ridiculous but kinda cute too, the way only little kids are. I can't help but laugh.

I set out two paper plates, grab four slices of white bread, spread two with peanut butter, then slather the other two with grape jelly. After I piece them together, I cut the crusts off mine. I hate crusts. I love the soft, airy white part in the middle of the bread.

If Sam were here, I couldn't do this. I did one time, and he about broke my arm, forcing me to eat the crusts. But he's not here. So I do what I want.

Though when I toss the crusts in the trash, I make sure to cover them up so he doesn't see.

When I put the sandwiches on the table, I say, "Dinner is served!"

Ford's about to bite his sandwich when he sees mine. He looks at his, then looks back at mine.

I ask, "What?"

He says, "I don't like crusts either."

"Yes, you do. You eat them all the time."

"Nuh-uh. I don't."

"Ford, just eat."

"No! I don't like crusts!" Ford squeals.

"It's the exact same sandwich," I say. "Just with the crust. Now, eat it. You're a growing boy. You need all the food you can get."

"Nooooooo," he moans, throwing himself up and down, bucking in his chair.

I start laughing.

"Don't laugh at me!" he yells.

I can't help myself. Angrier than I mean to, I snap, "Don't yell at me!"

"I'm not eating this crap!" he yells again.

"Hey! Don't talk like that! Just eat your sandwich!" Now I'm yelling louder than him, like I'm trying to match Mom. I hate that I do this. I tell myself to calm down, 'cause I feel myself getting mad. Over a dumb sandwich.

That's when Ford hops down from his chair, and throws it against the wall.

Then I'm shouting, "Sit down! Now! You will eat that sandwich, and you will like it!" I hear myself, and I sound just like Sam, the way he talks to me. It makes me feel sick.

Ford swings back and hits me as hard as he can.

It doesn't hurt much, 'cause he's little. But it surprises me. 'Cause he's so angry. Like real angry. I can see it in his eyes.

In that moment, he looks like his dad.

He looks like our mom too.

I grab both his arms. And I shake him. I shake him hard— not to hurt him, to get his attention. But I'm shouting, "*No*. You *don't* do that. You *don't* hit me. Do you understand?! You and me? We do *not* hit people. We are *not* like them! OK? We can't be like Mom and Sam!"

I shake him again. His big wet eyes look at me, scared.

His scowl crumbles into tears. And then he's crying.

It feels like God punches me in the chest, 'cause suddenly I can't breathe. I wonder if I hurt him. If he'll remember this. If he'll hate me forever. All this guilt wells up inside me, like I ruined him. Like I broke him, the way I'm broken. And all the anger in me melts into regret. I did it again. I'm a monster. Ruining the world around me. Destroying everything I touch.

I wrap my arms around my little brother and hug him as gentle and tight as I can. I hold his small back, the back of his head, I hold him the way I wish I'd held my sister, even if just once. And I'm crying too. "I'm so sorry, Ford. I didn't mean to scare you. Are you hurt? Are you OK?"

He nods, but he's still crying. He asks, "Are you mad at me?"

"No. I'm not mad. I'm not mad at you, Ford. But you can't hit people, OK?" I hold him for a long time, both of us crying, and I just keep saying, "We can't be like them. We can't. We have to be better."

radio

Mom drives. Not a cloud in sight. The Texas sky's the kind of blue that's real happy and light, 'cause it's midday. Halfway after sunrise and halfway 'til sunset. Real warm, but not hot. I hang my head out the window. I know I shouldn't, but I stare up at the sun til my eyes burn.

"I love this song!" Mom says, turning up the radio. "Nuthin' but a G Thang," by Dre and Snoop. Somehow, she knows all the words. I scrunch my face, embarrassed, even though it's just me and her in the car.

"Mom, stop. You're too old to sing this."

Outside the window, strip malls move past. I worry someone I go to high school with will see. Mom is rapping all the words in rhythm. She flashes a rare grin, dancing in the driver's seat from the waist up, bouncing her shoulders.

"You can't say the n-word!" I squeal. "You're white!"

"No, I'm Latina!" Mom says in her thickest accent, teeth on tongue.

I roll my eyes.

Mom's hand comes at me, pushing my shoulder. "Sing along with me. I know you know the words too."

I do, but I shake my head.

She nudges me again. "Come on."

We're running errands, the two of us. The post office. The library. Walmart. The grocery store. Maybe we'll even stop for lunch at Taco Bell, or Burger King.

It's just me and her. Like it was after my dad left, but before Sam. The only time we knew peace and quiet. My dad wasn't fighting with her in the trailer. Sam wasn't hitting her in our apartment. And Mom wasn't hitting me. Or lying on the floor crying. There was no screaming or tears or fists. Just her, the record player, and me.

I find myself singing along with her.

The smirk on Mom's face grows ear to ear. Her joy matches the sky. I find myself dancing too. We move our shoulders in unison, reciting the rhymes. The song goes by too fast. It ends. But next on the radio is Janet Jackson's "That's the Way Love Goes." Mom rolls into it. I follow. We're both singing, dancing, almost laughing—'til I pay attention to the lyrics.

About love being blind, about getting burned by it.

On my knee, a small round scar stares up at me, like an eye of fresh pink skin. It's the size and shape and color of the eraser end of a pencil. But it isn't cute like a pencil. 'Cause the scar was born from the end of a cigarette that Sam put out on my leg.

"Why?" I whisper.

Lost in the music, Mom sings. She doesn't hear me.

I turn off the radio.

"Hey! I was listening to—"

"Why are you with him?"

"With who?"

"Sam."

The car is quiet. Even with the wind blowing in from the windows down. In the distance, someone honks. A bird calls. Voices carry from a fast food drive-in. But the silence between Mom and me is thick. Like mud flooding over us.

Mom says, "It's complicated."

"Uncomplicate it for me."

Her mouth opens, but nothing comes out. It closes. When it opens again, she says, "You wouldn't understand. You're not old enough."

"I'm older than I look," I say.

She says, "You've never been in love."

The distance between us isn't just the middle of the car. It isn't the cupholders, or the stick shift. It isn't the coins in the change dish. It's this great big canyon between us. She's on one side of understanding, and I'm on the other.

I say, "If you love someone, you don't hit them. You don't hurt them."

She says, "You're naïve."

After a long time of quiet, an eternity at a red light, she finally adds, "When you love someone, all you can do is hurt them."

A tremble starts in my chest, rattling upward, until it comes out on my lips with a quiver. "But you said he killed your daughter."

Mom looks at me, her eyes filled with empty confusion. "What are you talking about?"

It takes all my strength to even speak her name. It's heavy on my tongue, the way I imagine the world would be if you could weigh it on a god's golden scale. *"Marisa."*

Without missing a beat, Mom looks me in the eye, and says, "Who?"

glass

"Come on," Todd says, pushing up his bedroom window. He grabs two Halloween masks, tossing the skeleton one to me. "Bring that."

"Where we going?"

"Don't be a pussy." Todd unclicks the screen, lowers it to the ground. He hops out the window into the night. I follow through the bushes into his backyard. He puts on his mask.

"Can I be the vampire?"

"Just be the skeleton," he groans.

I put it on. I hate the thick plastic smell, my hot breath warming my face. The world feels tight and tiny, smothering. Like I'm under a blanket, underwater.

"What if your mom comes and checks on us?"

"Then she'll know we snuck out," he says. "Who cares?"

Todd pulls a pack of cigarettes out of his pocket. He puts one in his mouth and lights it. He takes a drag. In the dark, the vampire mask makes him look like a real vampire smoking. Todd holds the cigarette out for me.

I shake my head. "No thanks."

He rolls his eyes. "Scared?"

"No. I don't want cancer."

"Whatever."

We pass house after house, decorated with spooky decorations. Pumpkins on porches. Scarecrows guarding lawns. Webs and giant plastic spiders in trees. Foam tombstones that look real. I hate zombies, but part of me wishes a hand would punch its way through the grass. My life would make a little more sense if evil were real, something I could hit.

Todd flicks the cigarette butt out into the air. A tiny red spark twirls through the sky like a firefly. When it hits the ground, it sparks and goes out. Dead.

After a ten-minute walk, we turn onto a quiet street. The darkness is thick, but shies away from the streetlamps along the empty street. There are no people. No cars. Just me and Todd and the wooden bones of houses being built.

I ask, "What are we doing here?"

"You ask more questions than my girlfriend."

"I don't want to get arrested."

"Then shut up."

I follow Todd into a cul-de-sac, the half-made house farthest away from the sleeping neighbors. The front yard is all plastic-covered bricks, severed cords, forgotten tools, crushed cans, empty fast-food bags, and nails. The roof is done, some of the interior walls have pink fiber filler and pipes, but outside, the house is naked, like it forgot to wear its skin.

Todd walks up to the front door and jiggles the handle. He frowns dramatically. "Oh no. It's locked."

"Did you knock?"

"Good idea." Todd taps quietly on the door.

I walk through the open framing and around, to open the door, speaking through my mask. "Well, hello. May I help you?"

"I'm selling Bibles door-to-door."

"Wonderful. Won't you come in?" I bow, inviting the vampire inside.

"I don't mind if I do." Todd saunters in and looks around. "I like what you've done with the place."

"That's kind of you to say. What do you think of the, uh . . ."—Todd waits for a few seconds while I try to think of something funny to say—"the decorating?"

He rolls his eyes. "You suck."

"Your girlfriend sucks."

"Yeah, she does." Todd raises his hand for a high-five.

I shrug and walk past, leaving him hanging.

"You're a dick," Todd says. "I don't know why I hang out with you."

"Feeling's mutual. So why are we here?"

Todd takes off his mask, shoving it in his pocket. I do the same, relieved by the cool night air on my face.

Todd checks his watch. "Some guys are going to meet us in a few. They're going to drug you and steal your organs. They'll give me fifty bucks if I keep my mouth shut."

He's kidding, I know that. But some part of my brain isn't sure. My mind races, like at home when Mom and Sam fight. In a flash, I make note of a four-by-four wood block, a screwdriver, a box cutter, a hammer, and a nail gun. I check the front, the sides, the stairs, and the back of the house, over the fence. Weapons and escape.

Noticing my face, Todd says, "I was joking."

"Duh," I say. "Like you know anyone cool enough to do that."

"I do."

Now I roll my eyes. I've known Todd since fifth grade. He talks a big game, but the only things he's good at are skateboarding, looking cool, and pissing off girls.

"Here we are."

We're standing in a large room in the back of the house. One day it'll be a dining room. Right now, it's whatever we want it to be. The room opens onto a backyard, piled with building materials on pallets. Todd hands me a brick.

I hand it back. "I'm good. Stealing bricks doesn't do anything for me."

"We're not stealing shit," Todd says. He points to a wall. Leaning against it is plate after plate of glass. He takes the first one off the top and leans it against a support stud. He takes the brick out of my hand, rears back, and launches it.

The glass shatters, hundreds of shards crashing onto the bare concrete floor, the tinkling sounds vibrating all around us. Some of the glass bits catch the moonlight, just-so, and light up like diamonds.

The breaking glass shakes something loose in me. I flinch, shuddering violently. Then shout, "Jesus! Fuck, Todd! The neighbors are gonna call the cops."

Todd shakes his head. Through the new cigarette in between his teeth, he says, "We're far off. They won't hear shit. If they do, we'll see the pig cars coming, and vamoose." Todd takes another plate of glass and moves it into place. Glass cracks and breaks under his boots. He takes another brick off the pile and holds it out for me.

I hesitate. So he goes again.

He throws it, harder this time. The pane of glass explodes into a million little pieces. In the darkness, the sounds are amplified. An old memory tries to force its way to the front of my mind. I shove it back, the way bigger kids shove me around at school. Still, I can't help closing my eyes, my whole body tensing up.

Todd asks me, "What's up?"

"I hate the sound of breaking glass."

"Why?" he asks, pulling another pane of glass into range.

I try not to look at the memory too closely. Just a glance. "When I was a kid, maybe six or seven, I saw a guy throw a woman into a window. Her arm went through, and this big shard went in her arm. When she pulled it out"—I take a breath, and push it away—"there was so much blood."

"Cool," Todd says. He picks up another brick. "If you hate the sound, take it back."

"Take it back?"

"Yeah. Instead of hating it, *love* it. The glass isn't breaking you. *You're* breaking it." Todd holds the brick out for me.

I think of the blood. The brightest red I've ever seen. Like a balloon in your hand, before you let go, and it floats up into the sky, never to return.

I think of my mom saying "*Who?*" when I brought up Marisa. As if it never happened.

As if I made it up. Imagined it. Did I imagine it? Am I crazy? I can't even talk about it with anybody.

Not with Mom

Not with Sam.

Ford's too young.

Who would even listen?

The brick sits in Todd's hand, staring at me.

So I take it.

In my hand, the brick feels heavy and light at the same time. When I squeeze, it doesn't give. It's solid. Hard. Invulnerable. Not like flesh. Glass can't hurt a brick.

So I throw it as hard as I can.

The sound of shattering echoes through the empty house.

"That's the spirit," Todd says, grinning.

My conscience comes up. "Aren't we destroying someone's property?"

"Nah," Todd says. "Companies build houses. No one's bought this yet. So we're just breaking glass some big corporation can buy again. No one gets hurt. Harmless fun."

This time, I line up two panels of glass. I pick up another brick.

The old memory stares at me: Sam and Mom's first fight, the first I saw anyway. Him shoving her, her elbow smashing through the dining-room window, the bright crimson running down her arm. I stare back at the memory. But this time, I have a brick in my hand.

I throw.

I throw it away from me. The memory and the brick.

Again and again, until the sound of breaking glass doesn't make me cringe.

Then we hear the siren. Red and blue lights flash as the police car pulls into the driveway. I'm surprised to hear my own laughter when Todd pales and freezes. I grab him by the collar and yank him toward the back. He follows me, as I run the path I mapped out earlier. Onto one pallet of bricks, leaping onto the next, then to the eight foot fence, leap, climb over, drop, and run.

Todd and I race until we can't anymore. Then we hide behind trees and laugh and laugh and laugh. We're still laughing long after we crawl back through his window.

snow globe

"Of course it would rain today," Mom sneers. Her fingers grip the steering wheel so tight, they turn white. Mom leans forward, trying to see through the foggy front windshield.

"Here." I hit the De-Fog button. Heat stutters and coughs out the little vents, slowly revealing the rainy highway ahead.

"How'd you know how to do that?" Mom asks, laughter in her voice. "You're so smart."

I shrug. She's being nice. But it feels like a trick. Like a bear trap, waiting for me to step in it.

Our little Toyota Tercel hatchback speeds toward Abilene. Raindrops skitter along the windows like tiny transparent trains having seizures. I trace my finger alongside them until they pass off the glass and disappear from view.

Mom asks, "Excited to see Abuela?"

"Are you?" I ask.

If she hears, she ignores me.

"We're too far from DFW to get the city radio stations. Want to try and get a local one?"

I shake my head no.

"Someone's a Gloomy Gus," Mom says, this big Julia Roberts smile painted on her face. Usually I'd be happy to see it. But's it's been over a week of Mom's over-the-top excitement and laughter and bouncy new self. Which means any second she'll crash and everything around her will get burned.

"Why so gloomy, Gloomy Gus?" Mom asks.

I shrug.

"Gloomy *Bus*," Ford says, pointing out the window as a Greyhound passes by.

Madonna's "Vogue" comes on the radio. Mom turns up the volume. She starts singing along. I want to join, but any little thing could set her off. It's better if I just sit here and don't do anything at all.

The gray sky is still pouring down on the world when we enter Abilene city limits. We pull off the highway and onto Vogel Avenue. Mom slows, then stops. In front of us, a dip in the road has turned into a wide stream. Brown water races past, filled with grass and twigs and tree branches and trash.

Ford takes off his seat belt and leans forward over my shoulder so he can see. "*Whoa*."

I say, "That's not good."

Mom asks, "How deep do you think that is?"

"Three or four feet."

"No way," Mom says. "I don't remember that."

"It is." I point to the street sign that says DIP to help my argument. "We should turn around."

"We'll be fine."

"Let's find another way."

"I'm tired of driving. We've been in this car for three hours. Come on, let's have an adventure."

Mom shifts into drive and taps the gas. The car rolls forward. The water rises inch by inch at the door. First slow, then fast. Too fast. Murky water splashes at the window. The engine stops. The whole car jostles left, pushed by the current. Ford and Mom scream as water swirls up from beneath, rising from the floorboards, soaking our shoes. My mind flashes to every submarine movie I've ever watched. I don't want to drown.

I remind myself that the stream outside is only a few feet deep. That it's rainwater, meaning no alligators, no sharks. That I'm an excellent swimmer. That we're only a few blocks from Abuela's house. That this is hardly the most scared I've ever been.

"What do we do?" Mom screams.

"Here's the plan," I say, hardly recognizing the authority in my voice. "Don't open your door, or the whole car will flood. Instead, I'll roll down my window, and we'll climb out, one at a time. Then we go to Abuela's and call a tow truck."

"But the car—"

"Isn't going anywhere." I roll down the window. Water splashes at the edge. I hesitate in the window frame, then slip my legs into the dirty waters. The river swirls around my waist, a few inches higher, then stops. It's colder than expected, but I'm laughing. "Ford, come here."

My little brother crawls into my arms, clinging to me like a magnetic koala baby. He squeals, "Don't let me go!"

"I won't. I promise."

Mom's shrieking rises and falls like a roller coaster as she follows. I wait, holding my hand out for hers. "Grab our bags."

Mom splashes around inside the tiny hatchback, then comes out, desperately gripping my hand. I lead the way forward, one leg sloshing after the other. The water gets shallower.

I take a second to look around. I've been to Abilene dozens of times. I was born here. But I've never seen it like this. With rain pouring so hard, the nearby park turned into a shallow lake, our car half underwater, and me with Ford in my arms, Mom trailing behind us, and me—like Indiana Jones leading the way to safety.

When we see Abuela's house, we break into a run. It's a joyous jog. We're all laughing, clothes soaked to the bone, hair sliding down into our faces. As I ring the bell, *ding-dong*, Mom and I look at each other. She hugs me. "We survived!"

I repeat, "We survived!"

When Abuela opens the door, her face is pure terror, until it's eased by our laughter. "¿Que pasó?" she asks again and again, as she ushers us inside, into warm showers and electric blankets and her loving arms.

I've told the story four times already. First to Abuela, then to the tow-truck guy, then to Abuela again, then to my aunt Francesca and her son, Donald. When my cousin asks to hear it again, I don't hesitate. The whites of Donald's eyes grow when I get to the part where we have to forge through the brown river.

"You're a hero," Francesca says, rubbing my back.

"You think so?"

"You were brave during the worst of it," she said. "Most people wouldn't know what to do. I wouldn't. Right, Luciana?"

Mom grabs my hand, squeezing it. Proud.

"That's so wild," Donald says.

The four of us, and Ford, are sitting around Abuela's dining-room table. I'm fingering a tear in the yellow picnic-plaid plastic tablecloth. Abuela is busying herself in the kitchen, preparing another round of hot chocolate. She won't stop putting blankets and towels over me and Ford. Her accent as thick as the afghan, she says, "You have to stay warm, or you'll catch cold."

"They're fine, Mamá," Mom says. She is drying her hair with a towel, dressed in Abuela's robe and slippers. "We're all fine."

"Yeah, we survived," I say. Mom and I exchange a glance. She high-fives me. "I'm never going to forget today."

"Me either," Ford says.

"Did anything like this ever happen to you when you were little?" I ask my mom and her sister.

"We traveled all over when your grandfather was in the military," Aunt Francesca says, "We lived in Kansas, Alaska, Africa—"

"You lived in Africa?!" I ask Mom. "I didn't know that!"

Mom shrugs. "It was a long time ago."

Francesca smiles at my mom. "I have a story—about you. Remember when we were living in Tripoli, Libya? On the bus, going to school?"

Mom shakes her head, confused.

Francesca continues, "There was this girl at our school. She was always mean to everyone, especially your mom. One day, she gets on the bus and pulls your mom's hair as she walks by. Well, I guess Luciana had enough. Your mom stood up and called her a nasty name. All the kids laughed . . .

"Except the girl's brother. He was holding a lunchbox—and back then, lunchboxes were made with metal—and he swung it, and *Wham!* He hit Luciana up the side of her head. There was blood everywhere. The bus driver turned around and drove us back home. I was holding your mom's head, trying to stop the bleeding."

"I remember," Abuela says. "I had to call a neighbor to drive us to the nearest hospital. The base was thirty minutes away. Luciana had to get seventeen stitches."

Donald winces. Abuela shakes her head. Francesca giggles. I look at Mom. She's smiling, but not a real smile. It's forced. Her teeth are gritted together. "I don't remember any of that."

"How could you forget?" I ask.

"I just . . . don't." Mom gets this empty, far-away look in her eyes. Like she's somewhere else. "But if Francesca and Mamá say it happened, then I guess it did."

Mom starts drying her hair with the towel again and walks back toward the guest room. I follow. "Mom, you OK?"

She turns around. For a second, it's like she doesn't recognize me. She shakes her head. "Why would someone want to remember something unhappy? Not me. Better to just forget it and never think of it again."

The next day, we go to Dyess Air Force Base to see the jets. Old planes that got decommissioned and set up so kids can climb on them and sit in the seats. I did it when I was little. Ford loves it now. Donald too. The three of us run around, arms out like planes, shooting at each other. Francesca asks Mom, "Have you seen the new construction?" They walk to the edge of the park to look.

Abuela is sitting alone on a park bench watching her grand-children. This might be the only time I get her alone, and I have to ask. It takes a few minutes to build up my courage. My palms are sweating. I'm real nervous. Finally, I say, "Can I ask you a question?"

"Por supuesto," Abuela says. "You can ask me anything."

I stare at the ground. At the dirt and a few scattered pebbles. The little green blades of grass trying so hard to reach up toward the pale sky.

The question sits on my tongue, heavy, refusing to leave my mouth. For weeks, I've been wondering if I made up everything about my sister in my head. Mom doesn't remember. But maybe she doesn't want to remember. Maybe she can't.

"What is it, mijo?"

I'm almost too scared to ask. Like I can't breathe until I do.

"When I was seven . . . did I . . . did I have a sister?"

Nearby, a bird takes flight. Abuela flinches. I wonder if it's because of the bird or my question.

"I . . . when I came back from Tennessee one summer, Mom told me . . . she told me I had a sister. That she . . . you know . . . that she died."

Abuela stares out across the field.

"And I see it, all of it, so clearly in my head. These super-vivid memories, but I don't know if they're real, 'cause I brought it up and Mom didn't know what I was talking about. It made me feel crazy. But then yesterday, when we talked about Africa, she didn't know that either, so maybe, maybe she forgets a lot of stuff? Maybe Mom has some kind of amnesia, like in comic books. I don't know. But I need to, 'cause I think . . . I know I had a sister but she . . . I never got to meet her. So at the very least, I need to remember her, 'cause someone needs to. 'Cause if she was real, she deserves that, to be remembered I mean. So . . . is she? Is she real?"

From under her glasses, a tear escapes down Abuela's cheek. "She told you?"

I nod my head.

"I told her not to. Not even before. Sometimes these things, they go badly . . . and her relationship with Sam was . . ." Abuela sniffles, still staring out at the field. "Why would she tell you? You were just a little boy."

"But it was—" I start. Then my voice fails. I can't say it. That it was *my fault*.

Not to Abuela. I don't want her to know. To hate me, the way Mom hates me.

"So Marisa was real?"

Abuela nods. "Yes." Another tear falls. Abuela takes a tissue from her purse and wipes it away. "She would have been a beautiful little girl. Mi primera nieta."

Relief washes over me, that I was right. That I hadn't imagined it. But at the same time, this pit opens up in my stomach. I didn't mean to upset Abuela. I take her hand. "I'm sorry. I shouldn't have brought it up."

Her soft, wrinkled hand squeezes mine. "You should have. You can ask me anything. I will tell you the truth. I am always here for you. Siempre."

On Saturday, Abuela takes us back to the Dyess Air Force Base. We go to the commissary first, to buy groceries. Then we go to the exchange. Abuela buys Ford and me some clothes. We even look at furniture. Somehow, Abuela talks Mom into letting her buy some furniture for our apartment. Ford and I are getting bunk beds. That means no more sleeping in a sleeping bag on the floor.

After, we go to the mall and eat Chick-fil-A, my favorite. Abuela buys me new shoes. Then we have dinner with my cousin and aunt. Donald and I build LEGO spaceships while Mom and Francesca catch up.

On Sunday, we find out the car is still getting fixed and needs another day. It isn't broken or anything, but the engine is still wet I guess. So we go to the movies. Donald and I really want to see *Bram Stoker's Dracula* or *Home Alone 2*, but Ford pitches this big hissy fit 'cause he wants to watch Disney's *Aladdin*, so we have to see that instead.

Then it's Monday.

"The visits always go by too fast," Abuela says. She hugs me again and again. Then kisses me right in the ear, making it pop. I used to hate it, but now it makes me laugh.

Francesca and Donald wave. Mom runs over and gives Francesca another hug. When Mom's around her sister, she laughs a lot more. They whisper a lot, especially about Abuela. They roll their eyes and giggle when they don't think anybody is watching. But I see it. And I'm glad. 'Cause Mom seems younger. Almost like my age.

But when Mom slides into the driver's seat, and says, "Time to go home," all that youth drains away. She's herself again. I wonder if it's 'cause she has to go back to work, or go back to Sam.

I take a chance and say, "We could stay."

"What?"

"Abuela would love if we stayed. She has two guest rooms.

One for you, and one for me and Ford. We could go to school here. We'd spend more time with Francesca and—"

Mom shakes her head. "Don't be silly. Sam is waiting for us."

Without the rain, the drive takes two and a half hours, which feels like forever.

Fifteen minutes in, Ford is already passed out in the backseat. I'm glad it's not raining. After we leave Abilene, the sky gets all blue and the sun comes out.

Looking at my window, I see a fingerprint trail, dragged along the window. It's mine. From five days ago. It seems like all that happened a long time ago.

"Remember when you thought it was safe to drive through the water?"

"People make mistakes."

"I'll never forget it," I say. A moment later, I ask, "What's your favorite memory? From when you were my age?"

"I don't know," Mom says.

"Pick one. Anything."

"I don't remember."

"You have to remember something."

Even though it's not raining, and the windshield isn't foggy, Mom leans forward and grips the steering wheel a lot harder. "I don't though."

"You don't have *any* memories from your childhood? None?"

Mom doesn't move. She's so still, I wonder if she's breathing. If her heart is beating. If she were anyone else, I might risk touching her, to see. But my fingers stay in my lap.

Outside, the Texas hill country rolls up and down, like roller coasters with no one on them. Sometimes I see a horse in the distance. Sometimes a lone house, out there in the middle of nowhere, all by itself. Abandoned.

"I have one," Mom finally says. "When we lived in Alaska. I was little, maybe five or six. For Christmas, our teacher got all of her students a little snow globe. It was the most beautiful thing I'd ever seen. I couldn't wait to show my brothers and sisters. It snowed the whole day. Walking home, I noticed that everything was white, blanketed with two feet of snow. When I got home, I looked in my backpack and the snow globe was gone. I searched everywhere, but it wasn't in our house. So I went outside, to search for it, to retrace the walk home. More and more snow fell, and then there was a big blizzard . . ."

Mom's voice trails off.

A minute passes. The car feels cold as I imagine Alaska, my mom out there looking by herself in the dark. I imagine Mom the way I sometimes imagine my sister as five or six years old. My little mom, in a blue parka, desperately searching for something in the snow that she can't find. I think of my mom's tears, and wonder if they froze.

"And?" I ask. "Did you ever find the snow globe?"

Mom shakes her head. Her stare is vacant. "No. I never saw it again."

cans

"H-h-he's h-here." Sam's hands shake as he looks out the blinds. "B-b-boys, b-be on y-your b-b-best b-behavior. P-p-please. R-r-rex, L-l-luciana, d-don't t-tell h-him I g-got f-fired."

"Fired?" I ask. "You said you *quit* your job."

"J-j-just *d-d-don't* b-bring it u-u-up!"

Ford's on the tips of his toes, trying to see out the window. I pick him up and we both peek. Mom doesn't get off the couch. Instead, she rolls her eyes, crosses her arms, and adds, "Here we go. Another shitty Thanksgiving."

Outside, a beat-up gold VW Bug pulls into a parking space. It makes it halfway in, at an angle, then stops short. *Bang!*

All of us jump. "Was that a gun?"

"No. That was the sound of Luther's piece-of-shit car backfiring," Mom says.

"L-l-let's g-g-go." Sam's stutter is worse than usual. Like his dad coming to visit is terrifying.

In the driver's seat, Luther is finishing off his beer. Done, he crushes the aluminum can and tosses it over his shoulder. When he opens his door, a couple of empty cans spill out onto the pavement. *Clank-clatter-clink.*

Luther teeters. Sam tries to help, but his dad swats him away. The old man leans against his car door for support, smelling like an ashtray. He's fifty-six, but looks eighty. A trucker cap sits on his head, a salt-and-pepper handlebar mustache dropping off his chin. Too-tanned skin hangs on his skeleton like a damp bar rag. His leathery arms are covered with faded tattoos and splotches. His pearl-buttoned cowboy shirt is stained, tucked into tight jeans that suck close to his long, lean legs that meet the ground with cowboy boots.

Sam says, "H-h-hey, D-d-dad."

Luther ignores him. "Where's that grandson o' mine? Not you," he says to me, "the one that's mine by blood."

Ford peeks out from behind my thighs.

"Come here, boy!" Half the teeth are missing from Luther's smile. The others are stained yellow or smeared in chewing tobacco. He spits a thick brown loogie on the ground. "Don't be scared, Shelton, get over here."

"It's Ford," I note.

Luther snarls at me. "That's wha' I said."

"G-g-go on, Ford. Th-that's y-your paw-paw."

Ford steps forward, but holds my hand like a safety line.

Luther rolls his eyes, walks over, and yanks Ford away from me. "Don't be a sissy, boy. Holding hands is for girls."

"He's *not* a sissy, he's a little kid," I snap. Sixty seconds, and already I'm pissed off. I step forward to pull Ford back from the drunk, but Sam gives me a warning look.

Luther either doesn't hear me, or doesn't care. He's talking at Ford, who looks back at me.

"I-i-it's OK," Sam says, "th-this's y-your g-grandpappy."

"He is?" Ford asks.

"Kid's a hoot," Luther snorts. His lanky torso disappears through the car window, almost falls in, then stumbles out with a plastic pharmacy bag. He gives it to Ford. "For your birthday."

Through gritted teeth, I say, "It's November. Ford's birthday is in April."

My brother pulls out a red-and-yellow plastic truck. There's a big sticker on it reading, SALE: 50% OFF. Ford says, "It's missing a wheel."

Luther ignores him and walks over to me. He acts like he's going to slug me, but stops at the last possible second. "Gotcha! How you doin', Rip?"

"Great." He never gets my name right. But I never correct him. Instead, I count how many different names he calls me in a visit. His record is four.

"Want some chew?" He offers a round plastic container from his back pocket. The lid has an image of a Native American Indian. Inside are black tufts of smokeless tobacco.

"No, thanks."

"He's too young, Luther," Mom says, arms crossed.

"Luciana. Always a pleasure." Luther goes to kiss her on the lips. Mom yanks her head back and sneers.

"W-w-wanna c-c-come i-i-inside?" Sam asks.

Luther answers, "You got beer?"

"We have Kool-Aid," Mom says.

Luther clears his throat, hocking another loogie on the sidewalk. Somehow, it looks grosser than bird poop.

Ford and I stay in the living room, playing with his Power Rangers figures, but periodically look up to see the adults at the dining-room table, chatting. Mom looks annoyed. Sam can barely look up from his hands. Luther talks about the weather, about work. When Luther pulls up a cigarette and a lighter, Mom snaps, "You can't smoke in here." Luther scowls at Sam, who scowls at Mom like she'll submit. Instead, she adds, "If he has to smoke so bad, he can go outside—like you do."

Sam and his father shuffle outside, Luther muttering under his breath.

I ask Mom, "How long is he staying?"

"One night," she says. "He's gone tomorrow after Thanksgiving lunch."

"That's what you said last time. And he stayed two weeks—in *my* room. After he left, my sleeping bag smelled like cigarettes for a year."

When Sam and his father come back inside, Luther says, "I'm hungry."

Mom shrugs. "So?"

"What're you cooking for dinner?" Luther asks.

As loud as she can, Mom goes, "Ha!"

Sam's face turns red. "W-w-we'll e-eat out. W-where sh-should we g-go?"

Mom shrugs. "Rex, why don't you and Luther go pick up some McDonald's? I'll give you cash."

I say, "No, thanks."

"It wasn't actually a question. You're going," Mom says. She pulls a roll of dollar bills from her purse. "Luther can drive. You know how to get—"

"No way!" I say. "I'm *not* getting in a car with him. He's wasted."

Sam's pissed 'cause I shamed him in front of his dad. Mom's pissed 'cause she's not in control. I don't care though. Every other Texas ad shows an overturned vehicle surrounded by ambulances. The tagline, "Don't Drink and Drive," is burned into my brain permanently. They bring it up at school all the time. Especially since a senior at our school died last year.

"You'll do as you're told," Mom snaps. She grabs for me, but I hop away, like a rabbit from a wolf. She makes another grab for me. I leap behind the velvet chair, using it as a shield. "You seriously want me to get in the car with him? That man's as drunk as a skunk."

Ford laughs, repeating, "Drunk skunk! Skunk drunk!"

Luther stands, his crooked finger unable to point at me as he shouts, "I ain't drunk! Who the fuck you think you are, Rick?! Talkin' ta me like—" He trips over his own chair and falls.

Sam goes to help, but his father takes a swing at him. "Little punk, I'm gonna kick his scrawny ass—"

"You're welcome to try," I shout, grabbing my brother and running into our room. I lock the door. I jam a textbook under the door to hold it firm. I sit, back against the door, for good measure. They can't get in now.

"Open this goddamn door!" Mom screams, slapping her hand against it.

"If you think he's safe to ride with, then one of you do it," I shout through the door. "Ford and I are staying here."

Ford's laughing up a storm, repeating, "Drunk skunk! Skunk drunk!"

Our parents are yelling from the other side. Someone kicks, and the whole wall shakes. But the door doesn't budge. I make a face at Ford, so he laughs harder.

"R-r-rex, g-goddammit!" Sam stutters.

"You are grounded!" Mom adds.

"Better grounded than dead," I shout back, adding, "Ford and I will both take a Happy Meal. Thanks."

My brother's face turns serious. "I want a cheeseburger."

"Ford wants a cheeseburger. I'll take the chicken nuggets. Maybe a baked apple pie?"

Ford asks me, "Can I have your Happy Meal toy?"

I answer honestly, "Depends on what it is."

Ford and I heard Sam and Luther leave an hour ago, but we're still waiting in our room. Ford's stomach growls. "I'm hungry."

"Me too," I say. "Where are they?"

The phone rings.

"Rex, answer that!" Mom shouts from somewhere on the other side of my bedroom door.

"Not until you promise you won't hit me. Or smack me, or pinch me, or any of that stuff. No kicking either. Oh, and promise I'm not grounded."

The phone rings again.

"Goddammit, Rex, the phone!"

I say, "There's a phone in the kitchen too, you know."

"*REX!*"

I pick up the line in my room. "Ogle-Schmidt residence. How may I direct your call?"

"P-p-put y-y-your m-m-mother o-on," Sam says.

"Mom! It's for you," I shout.

"Who is it?" Mom shouts back.

"Prince Charming!"

I hear the toilet flush, the bathroom door open, then Mom stomp down the hall. She slaps my door on the way. She answers the phone in the kitchen. "Rex, hang up," she says. I press the button on the phone once, but stay on the line. I put my hand over the receiver, and listen.

"Sam, where are you?" Mom asks.

"Th-there w-was an a-accident."

"Are you OK?"

"Y-yeah. D-dad d-d-drove into a-a p-parked c-car."

"Ha!" I laugh. "Told you!"

fever

don't feel well. I can't seem to get out of bed.

Last night, I tossed and turned all night. My body was aching and every time I swallowed, just my own spit, it burned like piping-hot coffee. It's the same now. Everything hurts and I'm real tired.

My bedroom window is open. Outside birds are chirping, grasshoppers are jumping around, there's a blue sky with a cool breeze. Inside my throat, it feels like a desert canyon, baking under the sun. My muscles feel tight but tired. And I'm hungry and thirsty and at the same time, I don't want anything.

"Come on, you're going to be late for school," Mom says from my door.

I shake my head. "I don't feel good."

Mom rolls her eyes, then disappears from the door. I guess I fall asleep, 'cause she comes back and she's real irritated. Her voice is shrill. "Why aren't you up yet?! I need to get Ford to—"

When she pulls back the cover and sees, something in her

face shifts. It softens. She puts the back of her hand on my forehead. "You're warm."

"My throat hurts."

"Well, if you want to stay home, be my guest. But I can't take care of you. I have errands to run and work—"

I don't know what else she says 'cause I fall back asleep.

When I wake up, the clock says seven. I'm confused 'cause the sun isn't up. It's dark out. It takes me a full minute to remember this morning, waking and talking to Mom and going back to sleep. Then all day, in and out of sleep, nightmares. At some point, Mom delivered me her cure-all: orange Gatorade and saltine crackers. Each bite, each slurp, was like a thousand black wasps stinging my esophagus all over.

I didn't go to school.

Everything from the back of my tongue down the well of my throat feels like magma—you know, the lava stuff under the earth—burning and churning, melting anything it touches. I sit up and the room spins in circles. I grab the sheets and grip them to steady myself. I fall off the bed anyways. I take a deep breath and pull myself up.

I try the Gatorade, and it's like drinking acid. I need water. I'm so thirsty. And hungry. But I don't wanna eat the salty crackers. I don't want anything. My body feels all wrong. My skin is boiling and everything beneath the surface aches.

Outside my room, Sam is laughing with Ford. My little brother is acting like a lion, growling ferociously. On all fours, he bounds around the living room, hopping on and off the couch, then on and off the chair, swiping at Sam's legs with his little fingers like claws. His dad howls with laughter. I stumble out of the room, bracing myself against the wall. When he sees me, Ford hops over and snarls, swatting at me like a cat with a mouse.

"Roar! I slice you with my claws and you're bleeding and you're dead."

When I hear the word "dead," I think of how sick I am. How people die from things like the flu. Or maybe I have cancer. Or worse, maybe I have AIDS.

My thoughts spiral and spin until nausea hits my stomach like a baseball bat. 'Cause I feel like I really am dying. I run to the bathroom, barely in time. I'm over the toilet, vomiting. Anything that comes up is like broken glass tearing through my insides, slicing open the soft parts of my throat. Tears stream down my face as I heave and then heave again. Chunks of saltine crackers in a river of sports-drink-orange puke.

I collapse onto my hands and knees and grab the bowl for support. I heave again, and the tears burn my eyes. When I'm done, I'm trying not to sob, but it all hurts so bad. Weak, I lay my head on the toilet rim. The cold porcelain feels nice against my blazing skin. I don't care about the bits and pieces of whatever I ate on my chin or on my shirt.

"Y-y-you l-l-look like sh-shit," Sam says from the bathroom door, keeping his distance.

"I feel like it too." Another wave of nausea comes over me. I heave. Nothing comes up. False alarm. I wipe the chunks from my lip with the back of my arm. I don't care what I look like. I just want to feel better.

"I'm t-taking your brother out f-for some d-dinner. You w-want anything?"

I shake my head. "No."

Ford appears behind Sam's leg. My brother drops the lion act and looks at me. His eyes well up. "Did I hurt you? With my claws? It was just pretend."

I shake my head again. "I'm just sick. I'll be OK."

"OK," Ford says.

I sit on the floor, holding the toilet. A few vomit aftershocks tremble through my body like mini-earthquakes. I belch this burning-hot acidic burp. Then I sink down onto the cool linoleum. Pressed against my face, I never realized I could love this floor so much. I notice the little green mat with its tufts of yarn. A clipped fingernail—or maybe one of Sam's giant toenails—lost and alone, under the cabinet overhang. Little dust bunnies, made of human hair. One lone, long hair slithers along one tile, trying to escape from my breath. I exhale again, and it tumbles and moves as if alive. It makes me think of the sand worms in *Dune*. The scope of the world changes, the hair grows in my mind until it's the size of a train. Then I wonder how large that makes me. I imagine myself a giant, as tall as a skyscraper. I wonder if maybe the world is just the body of a god, long dead.

My whole body freezes at the thought of death. Real terror floods through me. I'm crying, wondering if this is it. Then Marisa is there, brushing my hair back from my sweaty brow. She smiles, until I drift off to sleep.

The next thing I know, Sam is nudging my shoulder gently. "You sh-should sh-sh-shower off. Then get b-b-back in b-bed."

He closes the bathroom door. Through the thin door, I hear him tell Ford, "Y-you n-need to sleep in m-my room tonight. You d-don't want to c-catch whatever your brother has."

Usually I prefer hot showers, almost scalding. But tonight, I make it cold. The colder, the better. It washes over me, soothing my aching body. I can't stand up without getting dizzy, so I just sit in the shower letting it wash over me.

Night is the worst part. Alone in my room. Alone in the dark.

The shadows are thick and deep. Seeming alive in my half-asleep, half-waking state. Alive and evil. Full of demons. Come to punish or possess me. Or maybe they already have. Every muscle and joint contracts as though being ripped from the bone, aching with the heat that consumes me from the inside. My sheets are soaked, feeling icy when I move in them, or scalding hot when I don't move at all.

Or maybe the demons aren't in me yet. They're just waiting for me to expire. They're from hell, sent to drag me down to the fiery pits and eternal damnation for the things I've done. For the people I've hurt.

I think about my sister. How if I go to hell, I'll never see her again.

I start sobbing into my pillow.

Usually, Ford's little-kid snores irritate me. Now I miss them. I miss the comfort of having another person in the darkness with me. But I don't want him to feel the way I feel right now. I don't want anyone to feel like this. Not even Mom, not even Sam. This is true hell. This life right here. All the agony it brings with it. I want all the pain to end. But I'm terrified of what's waiting for me on the other side.

When I wake again, Mom's hand is on my forehead again. "Yeah, he's still hot," she whispers, but not to me. Sam is in my bedroom doorway. The room is only a little lit, 'cause the sun has just begun to come up.

"T-t-take him t-to the doctor," Sam says.

"And who's going to pay for it?" Mom says. "We don't have insurance."

"H-h-he's s-sick."

"It's just a little fever. He'll burn it off today. A few days' rest and he'll be fine."

Sam's lips tighten into a line.

"Mommy?" I try to turn my head, to look behind my pillow to see who said that. It takes half a minute to realize the voice was mine. "Mommy, can I . . . have some water?"

"Of course," she says. She gets up, pushes past Sam, and disappears. The kitchen is only ten feet from my bedroom door, but it seems to take a long time. My lids are heavy, so I close my eyes.

"Here you go." Something in Mom's voice is different. Gentle. She holds my head as I drink, like a little boy. She smiles. I wonder if I'm dreaming. But as soon as the tap water hits the back of my throat, it burns like boiling soup. I groan.

It's worse when the water hits my stomach.

Everything clenches, and I heave. "Huwghhhh." Mom thrusts my head into the mop bucket next to my bed just in time.

"S-s-see?" Sam says.

"He'll be fine," Mom says. "Kids get sick. Then they get better. That's what they do." She turns to me, and rubs my back a little. It feels nice. Foreign, but nice.

"Close your eyes, Rex. Get some sleep."

"Rex, can you sit up?" Mom says. "I need to go to work. You need to watch your brother."

"Huh?" I try to sit up. I get confused how the bunk beds got on the ceiling. My head throbs. I feel my heart beating throughout every inch of my body, like a hammer pounding. My throat is on fire. I touch it, feeling eggs just under the skin on either side of my swollen neck. I imagine the eggs are green, hard yet gelatinous, with small aliens growing inside. Mom is upside down. I shake my head, the room spins. White glares flare over my vision. When it goes normal finally, there are four of my mom, then three, and then just the one. She's wearing her waitress uniform.

"I have to go to work," she says. "Sam doesn't get home for three more hours. You need to watch your brother, OK?"

I nod, but already forget what she said.

"Come lay down in the living room."

My legs are made of lead. When Mom slides them over the bed's edge, they collapse to the carpet like heavy jelly. I can't tell if I'm crying or sweating. I don't know. Or care. It all hurts. Mom puts her arm around my waist, lets me lean against her. I rest my head on her shoulder, and it feels funny. Like a hug. No strings attached. Like characters in a sitcom with their moms. Except real. But then I'm confused. If it's TV people, then they're actors and it's not real.

Mom half-carries me, I half-drag my feet, to the living room. Ford sits in the pink chair watching cartoons until he sees me. His eyes widen.

"Here you go," Mom says, letting me fall against the couch. I am shivering head to toe. My teeth chatter so hard I think they'll shatter.

"So cold," I whisper. But that seems wrong, because I'm so hot. Why does everything hurt so much? Why is God punishing me?

Mom vanishes, reappearing with a handful of linens. She pushes a pillow under my head, covering me with a sheet and a crocheted blanket. Abuela made it for me. Or was it Grandma June? She's dead. I wonder if I'll see her soon.

My whole body hurts as I lie back, sinking into the couch.

Mom says to Ford, "Be good. Don't act up. Your brother is very sick. You have to help him by being good, OK? OK?"

Ford nods.

The front door closes after my mom. I see the cartoons on TV. *DuckTales*. I've seen this episode. My brother leans over the arm of the pink chair and stares at me. He asks softly, as if not wanting anyone to hear, "You OK?"

"Be good," I say, my throat scorched by every syllable. Then I pass out.

I've been swimming, I think. That's why I'm all wet. Soaked. It must be summer, too, because the sun is burning me. My whole body, even the insides. Want to turn over, or move into the cool shade under one of the public-pool umbrellas. Can't move though. So weak. Ears are ringing, must be a lifeguard, blowing his whistle. I wish he'd stop. Somewhere far away, Sam is calling me.

"Rex! Rex!" Sam is shaking me. Slapping my face. Seems about right, I think. "Rex, w-w-wake up!"

Sam pulls my eyes open. There is no sun. No public pool. I'm on our living-room couch. It's nighttime. Ford is crying.

"G-g-get up," Sam says. But he doesn't wait. He picks me up. "Ford, c-c-come on."

I'm floating. Levitation. I wonder if the fever is my super-power finally developing. All the pain was just a precursor to this. Telekinesis, or just flight? I don't care, I'm so happy. I want to be a hero, like the X-Men in my comics. Then we're outside. Stars in the sky. Jangle of keys. Sam hoists me into the passenger seat of the car. Ford sits in the back but holds my hand, squeezing it, his little fingers burn everywhere they touch. He's crying still.

"S'OK . . ." I whisper. "'m flying . . ."

The wind is in my face, powerful and cool. Streetlamps fly by, the lights melting and tracing behind. Sam runs a red light. Cars honk. The car stinks like old fast food. But the wind is pleasant.

"H-h-hang in there, Rex. Y-you're g-going to be OK. W-we're g-going to the h-h-h-hospital. You h-hear me? St-stay awake!"

I know I'm going to be OK. 'Cause now I have superpowers. No one will ever hurt me again. I try to say that, but for some reason I can't keep my eyes open.

"One hundred and six," Sam says. "The d-d-doctor said h-his temperature w-was 106."

"I didn't—I didn't know." Mom is crying. She's sitting at the end of the couch, her face buried in her hands. "I just—I kept thinking about how much it would cost to go to the doctor. Doctors are so expensive. Five minutes with them and you get a bill for three hundred bucks. And all they do is say, *Take aspirin and rest.*"

I'm under my grandma's crocheted blanket. My toes are stuck in one of the holes, a fish in the net. Usually that drives me nuts, but right now I don't care. I feel better.

"A r-r-regular doctor v-visit is three hundred. I h-had to

t-take him to the em-emergency room," Sam says. "That's g-gonna be m-more. A lot more."

"Why didn't you take him to urgent care?"

"B-b-because our kid was sick. I w-wasn't thinking."

I remember the IV in my arm. The doctor and the nurse fussing over me. Sam holding my hand and repeating, "I-i-it's g-gonna b-be OK now." The memory is like looking down a ten-foot pipe. But after the antibiotics, I could swallow water again. I didn't even throw it up.

Now I'm back home, on the couch. Ford is cuddled up next to me, his head on my stomach. I feel almost like me again. Weaker, but myself.

"We can't afford this," Mom says, crying. For once, she's upset, but not at me or Sam or Ford.

"W-w-we'll f-figure it out," Sam says.

"How? I can't get a second a job or we'll have to hire a baby-sitter for Ford. Then all our money will go to that."

Sam sits down and rubs his temples. Then he wrings his hands.

"I'm sorry," I say, my voice all raspy and scratchy, like a cartoon frog croaking the words. "I didn't mean to get sick."

Sam shakes his head. "N-not y-your fault. Sh-sh-shit happens."

"But the bills—" Mom started.

I interrupt. "Make my dad pay."

Mom raises her eyebrows.

"What's a thousand bucks to him?" I ask with my weird new voice. "Worst case, he'll have to take some time off the golf course at his country club. Or his wife will have to do without diamonds at Christmas. I know . . . a fate worse than death." My laughter turns into painful coughing.

Sam hands me a glass of water, then tussles my hair. "G-g-good idea."

A smile breaks on Mom's face. She wipes her tears. She leans over and hugs me. "I'm glad you're OK."

"Me too."

church

The day after Christmas is Sunday. Sam wakes me and Ford up early. "G-g-get up. G-g-get d-dressed."

After a rushed shower, I put on the pants and button-up shirt I wear on special occasions. The pants are way above my ankles, and I have to suck in my stomach to button them. My shirt is too tight too.

Sam calls me into the bathroom. He smells like cologne. He's freshly showered and shaven, wearing a dress shirt and tie. If I didn't know him, I'd think he was a businessman. Maybe a car salesman.

He hands me a tie. "P-p-put this on."

"I don't know how."

"Y-your d-dad n-never taught y-you?"

I shake my head.

Sam snorts, under his breath, adding, "T-t-typical."

Sam steps behind me in the bathroom. He pushes up my

collar, laying the navy tie around my neck. He reaches around, showing me. "O-over. U-under. Over. Through." He tightens the knot.

My stepdad smirks. He gives me a play punch in the arm. "Y-you look g-good."

When I come out, Mom says, "You look ridiculous. That tie's too big and everything else is too small. Just put on a tee and some jeans."

Sam growls. "He h-h-has t-to dress u-up for church."

"No, he doesn't," Mom snaps. "God understands we're poor. He doesn't care."

"W-well, m-my m-mother does. C-come on. We only s-see her this o-once or tw-twice a year."

Mom rolls her eyes, flinging herself onto the couch. She snatches a magazine from the carpet. I ask, "Aren't you going?"

"Hell no," she says. "Churches are full of hypocrites. They're racist and sexist and full of hate and greed. They say they want to help people, but no one's helping us."

"Can I stay too?"

Mom shrugs. "Sure. If Jesus wanted you to go to church, he'd call more."

I sit on the couch, taking my shoes off, when Ford comes out. He's wearing a pair of little-kid gray slacks, a white polo shirt, and suspenders. This is the cutest I've ever seen him. His big brown eyes. He stares at the shoe in my hand.

On the couch, Mom is flipping the magazine pages so hard, they tear. One falls to the ground, like a leaf from a dying tree.

I slip my foot back into my shoe.

———

The Dallas church is huge. Its parking lot goes on for a mile. Even though it's cool out, I'm sweating by the time we get to the front doors. Doris is standing there, as still as a statue.

When she sees Sam, she turns her cheek so he can kiss it.

"Did you find it OK?"

"Yes, m-ma'am," he says. My stepdad seems like a schoolboy for some reason.

Doris bends at the knee, opening her arms for Ford. It's the only movement where she doesn't move like a robot.

She wears spotless patent-leather shoes, tan stockings, a navy skirt, a blouse, and a button-up sweater. On it is a golden pin with Christ on the crucifix. Her hair is cut short, not a hair out of place. She shakes my hand as if we've just met, her arm rigid. I wonder if maybe she *is* a robot.

Inside, there are hundreds, maybe thousands, of people filling row after row of pews, like Scrabble tiles sliding into their little wooden racks. The whispers and excuse-mes and hello-how-are-yous all blend into a loud hum, like in the bleachers before a football game.

A hymn is led by the choir—a bunch of boys and girls in long dress robes, standing in front of a huge gold organ. The sermon's about the birth of Jesus, probably 'cause yesterday was Christmas. I know this story, how Mary was a virgin, she and Joseph had to travel, and they ended up at an inn and the three wise men came with gifts. It's a cool story, I guess, though I like Revelations better. And the part with the big flood, or David and Goliath.

I'm flipping through the Bible pages to find one of the stories I like, and Doris's hand grabs mine, squeezing it with more strength than I would have expected from an old lady. "Eyes front and center. And sit up straight." Even though she whispers, it's a command.

Sam glares at me.

Ford giggles, whispering, "You got in trouble."

Doris's eyes lock onto my brother. He straightens up too.

Looking at Sam, and looking at Doris, I can't figure it out. Her being his mother doesn't make sense. I definitely can't imagine her being married to Sam's dad.

Doris's car is as spotless as her clothes. There's not a speck of dust or a forgotten leaf on the floor. She insists she drive to lunch, and she'll drive us back to our car after. When Doris is driving, Sam doesn't talk. Even though we just left church, Doris turns the radio to another sermon. I guess she really likes religion.

As she pulls into a parking lot, Ford and I look outside. A giant, thick brown-and-white cow stands on a tall columned sign reading SIRLOIN STOCKADE. At the exact same time, my brother and I go, "YES!"

We love the family-style all-you-can-eat buffet, 'cause we can get whatever we want. Even though I always get the same thing. Ford follows me to the baked-potato station, where they have a pile of hot potatoes wrapped in foil. Using the tongs, I grab the biggest one. I cut it open, letting the steam roll up and out. I load it with way too much butter, shredded cheese, crunchy bacon bits, sour cream, and chives.

"Me too!" Ford says, so I do his the same way.

Sam says, "G-get a st-steak."

I shake my head. "I don't like steak."

"R-real m-men eat b-beef."

I shrug.

Back at the table, I add salt and pepper to my mountain of potato and dairy. Ford watches, then copies me.

When Doris sits, Ford and I both have our mouths full. She puts a napkin in her lap, and asks, "Did you already say a prayer, thanking the lord for your meal?"

I swallow the hot mouthful of scalding potato. "Oh. Sorry."

Ford leans forward and spits his mouthful out onto his plate.

"F-F—Ford!" Sam growls.

"It's hot," Ford says.

"Please bow your heads and take your neighbors' hands," Doris commands. We do. She prays. Ford puts my hand in his mouth and bites it. I snort, laughter bursting out. Not missing a beat, Doris squeezes my hand so hard, I nearly fall out of my chair. When she finishes with "Amen," she doesn't look at me or Ford or Sam. She picks up her knife and fork and starts cutting her steak with precision.

"You don't pray before you eat at home?"

Ford and I look at Sam. "I w-work l-late. Sometimes w-we d-don't e-eat t-together."

Doris turns on me. "Then it's your responsibility to raise Ford in the Christian way."

"But, um . . . I'm not though . . . I mean, I'm not *not* a Christian. I just . . . I'm not baptized. I've read the whole Bible though. And I read other stuff too. Like about Buddhism and Wicca. Oh, and the Qur'an—"

Doris drops her steak knife with a loud clank. "That's what terrorists read."

I shake my head. "No, it's not. Islam and Judaism and Christianity are all Abrahamic reli—"

"Not another word," she says. "I served in the U.S. Marine Corps. I think I would know better than a teenager."

Sam is glaring at me like I told her I worshipped Satan.

Doris takes a deep breath, touches the tiny gold cross around her neck. She picks up her silverware and starts over. To Sam, she asks, "Where are you working? Still doing lawn care?"

"N-no, ma'am. I g-got a n-new j-job. Dr-driving b-buses."

"City buses? As in public transportation?"

"I wish," I say. "He's driving a bus at my school."

"What's wrong with that?" Doris asks.

"I don't know. It's weird. No kid wants their stepdad working at their school."

Doris stares at me. "You think you're so enlightened reading heathen mythology. But if you were a good Christian child, you would applaud my son for an honest living."

I hadn't thought of it like that. Suddenly I do feel bad.

"Where is Luciana?" Doris asks Sam.

"She w-wasn't f-feeling w-well."

"Mom feels fine," Ford says, his mouth full of potato and sour cream. He shovels in another mouthful, then squeezes it through his teeth like a Play-Doh machine. "Mom doesn't like church people. She says they're hippo-cats."

Sam's face goes as red as the strawberry syrup at the dessert bar. Doris puts down her silverware and rubs her temples. I pinch my leg under the table as hard as I can, desperate to not burst into laughter.

Doris puts her hands together to pray. She's whispering so low I can barely hear over the sound of steak knives scraping against plates at other tables. Not until I hear her say, "First, she sends him to jail, and now she raises his only child with no care for his divine destiny under you—"

I ask, "Jail?"

Doris stops her prayer to look at me. "You don't know?"

"Who went to jail?"

Doris nods to her son. "Sam did. Because of what happened to your sister. But your mother is a liar. Why else would she drop the charges after a few days, and seduce him back into her bed?"

This new truth sinks in. How did I not know he went to jail? Why did Mom never tell me? Why did Sam never say anything? My thoughts are swirling out of control—

Then Ford says, "What sister?"

The whole restaurant—the buffet and the people and the smiling cartoon ice-cream cone over the frozen soft-serve machine—all of it goes crimson in my eyes. Like my eyes are bleeding, and I'm going to start screaming.

Ford doesn't know. And he doesn't need to know. And I don't want him to know. About Mom and Sam fighting, about me not being there, about Marisa—

My hands are shaking so hard I think it'll start an earthquake. I want to slap the food off the table. Throw the table over. I want to push Doris on the floor and scream at her to shut her mouth. Seeing us once a year does not make her part of this family. And she has no right to talk about my sister in front of my brother.

I want to. But I don't do any of it. 'Cause that's what Mom would do. And I'm not her. Instead, I swallow the anger down. I swallow it down, like I always do.

sock hands

Saturday morning, I lie in my bed. Tired. I was up late watching BBC's *Red Dwarf* on PBS while building a giant LEGO spaceship for Ford.

Ever since our lunch with Doris, I've been distracting Ford. When he remembers to ask about our sister, I tell him Doris made a mistake. I play it down. I think he's almost forgotten about what his grandmother said. One day I will tell him. But not yet. Not now.

I know she understands, sitting there, at the edge of my bed. Marisa nods, it's the right thing to do.

As I lay there, wanting my eyes to close, I can't stop wondering about Sam in jail. How did I not know? And should I ask? Should I bring it up? Would he tell me?

I yawn. I need to use the bathroom. I get up. But Mom's in there, cleaning. I know because the radio is playing and I hear the sound of a scrub brush brushing the tiles vigorously. Two oscillating fans bar the doorway, both on their high settings, blowing the smell of harsh chemicals out of the bathroom and into the rest of the apartment.

I say, "Mom, I need to go."

On her knees, over the toilet with a brush in her hand, she says, "So go outside. You're a guy."

"Seriously? I can't just pee in broad daylight."

"So go behind a tree."

"Can I just use the toilet?"

Mom stops scrubbing and looks at me. "You know I clean the bathroom every Saturday. If you needed to go, you should have gotten up earlier."

When I go to put on my shoes, Ford is watching Saturday-morning cartoons in the living room. Sam is pacing back and forth.

I ask, "You OK?"

"I n-n-need to t-t-take a dump!" Sam shouts.

From the bathroom, Mom shouts back. "Go use the bathroom at the pool building. I don't want you messing up my clean toilet."

Sam roars, and hits the front door with his fist. "A m-man sh-should be able to sh-shit in his own house."

"Only if he wants to clean the shit off the bowl after he's done! Every time you go, it's like a brown bomb goes off. What's wrong with you?"

Sam puts on his flip-flops and storms out of the apartment. Since he's using the bathroom for the pool next to our apartment, I have to walk to the other end of the complex to the other bathroom at the other pool.

For New Year's Eve dinner, Sam gives me a night off from cooking. He makes his favorite: sausage, boiled potatoes, and sauerkraut. We eat on paper plates. After, we toss everything into the trash. No dishwashing necessary.

Ford, Sam, and I move into the living room. Sam takes the pink velvet chair in front of the TV. I take the floor, using a couch cushion to prop up my head. Ford hops on the couch, where he usually sits with Mom.

Only, she doesn't join us yet. She has to clean the table. Not for us though, 'cause we honestly don't care that much. She does it for her. Like she needs the apartment to be clean, top to bottom. Not a hair in sight. No dust on any surface. Not a single crumb or sticky spot on the table.

First, Mom sprays down the dining area with Windex. Using four paper towels, she wipes the table spotless. Then she squirts it down again. She uses four new paper towels to clean it again. Depending on her mood, there's sometimes a third and fourth time.

Sometimes she goes through two or three bottles of Windex a week. Yet when she goes to the store, she never buys more than one bottle at a time. She goes to the store nearly every single day. Then she complains about it.

Mom isn't just this way with the kitchen table. She's this way with the kitchen, the bathroom, our bedrooms. Every day, she dusts, she vacuums, she cleans. And every day, she scowls at us, saying, "This place is a mess."

But it's not.

Tonight, she's on round six of wiping down the table.

"L-l-luciana," Sam says. "E-e-enough cleaning. W-we w-wanna start the movie."

Hands on hips, she inspects the table. "It's not coming clean."

"It's fine," I say.

She yells back, "It's not fine!"

I want to start the movie as much as Sam. So I get up, walk over to Mom. She's staring at the table. Not a streak on the surface. I ask, "Which part isn't clean?"

"All of it," she says, frustrated.

"Can I help?"

"No. You won't do it right. Just start the movie without me."

She unscrews the spray nozzle and pours Windex all over the table. She unrolls half the paper towel roll around her hand, like a glove, and wipes and wipes and wipes and wipes. She seems on the verge of tears.

"Mom, it's clean." I reach for her hand.

Her body is thirty-five years old, but looks younger. Her soft olive-skin is unblemished, no wrinkles. Her eyes look way too young, and at the same time, ancient. Though her hands remind me of a vulture's. The skin is hard, red, wrinkled, cracking in some places, like dry paint in a desert. Her obsession with cleaning is devouring her hands.

She pulls away from me, scurrying to the other side of the table. Bending down, she inspects. She spits on the table, scratching at it with her fingernails. "Why won't it come up?"

"There's nothing there," I say as gently as I can. "Let's watch the movie."

I guide her toward the couch, sitting her next to Ford. I turn off all the lights, so we're only illuminated by the TV. But all through the action and drama, Mom keeps looking over at the table. After, Ford asks, "What was your favorite part?"

"Of what?" she asks.

"The movie."

Mom says, "I don't know. I wasn't paying attention."

We turn off the VCR and switch it to the main channel, the one with the ball drop in New York City. It's only half an hour until midnight. Sam grabs another beer from the fridge. I pour ginger ale for me and Ford. As the world creeps toward a new year, minute by minute, Mom sits and stares away from the TV, toward the dining-room table.

After Ford's tucked in, after Sam's asleep, I read comics on the couch. Next to me, Mom quietly rubs lotion on her skin. After one coat, she adds another to her hands, slathering them until they're slick and moist. Then she covers them in Vaseline.

She says, "Rex."

I pick up the old pair of socks, and roll them up my mother's hands, wrists, and forearms. If the gloves were silk or leather, she might be a glamourous woman attending a ball. Instead, the yellowing cotton make her look like a baby that might scratch her own face if her nails aren't covered.

I say, "Happy New Year."

Her thin lips attempt to smile. They fail. She says, "Good night."

On her way to bed, she looks one last time at the table.

I wonder if she'll dream of the upcoming year. Or of the table. Or if she'll sleep at all.

running

We are fighting. It lasts a long time. Over an hour. I scream so loud it feels like my throat will always be raw. I can't do it anymore. I can't do this anymore. The fighting. The shouting. The waiting to get hit. I turn away from my mom, screaming, "I'm leaving."

"You can't go anywhere. You don't have a dime in your pocket. You'll freeze to death."

"I rather freeze than put up with you."

She swings. I dodge. I look her in the eye, so she can see my lips when she hears my words: "I'm done. I'm so done."

I run out the front door, snatching my shoes on the way. With all my strength, I slam the metal door as hard as I can. I turn and run. Out of the breezeway. Down the sidewalk. Behind me the door opens. Mom screams. "Get back here, Rex! Right fucking now!"

I'm one building away. Two buildings away. I hear her

shrieks, quieted only by the distance. "You'll be back! And you'll be sorry!"

My feet carry me forward. I don't stop running, not even when my skin tears on a jagged crack in the sidewalk. Three buildings away, four buildings, five . . .

I look back over my shoulder, in case Luciana is chasing me. She's not. Not this time. But I've left a trail. Three toes and the upper pad of my footprint, marked by blood. As soon as I notice, I leap off the sidewalk and into the grass. I run until I get to the other side of the Morrigan Place apartment complex. I find a nook between an air-conditioning unit and a fence. I duck behind to put on my shoes. I don't have socks. My right foot goes in dry, but my left foot is bleeding furiously. It could get infected. I don't care.

The foot is shoved in, smearing my old white sneaker with crimson. I stand, and start moving. Every step is agony. I don't even know where I'm going, but I have to go. I have to move. I can't go back.

There's this weight on my chest, I can't take a deep breath. This tension in my back, like my muscles are going to rip open. It's cold out, but I can't feel it. My skin is hot. My brain feels like it's on fire. Like there's a demon inside me, straight from hell, burning to get out. I think of fighting my mom. Of hitting her the way she hits me. Of fighting Sam. I'm not strong enough, but maybe if I let the monster in me do it. All those dark thoughts I carry around. If they could take shape, form into a beast that I could unleash. Maybe if I ripped away my face, you'd see it beneath.

I'm only halfway up Cattle Drive when I have to step off the road, into the tall grass, and throw up. Some part of me expects fire to come out. Or blood and organs. But it's just breakfast.

Half-digested Cheerios and milk. It looks wrong, splashed there in the grass. Like it doesn't belong. My brow wet, my whole hunched body soaked with sweat.

I straighten and start walking.

I can call Abuela. She'll come get me. Or my dad. Maybe I could go live with him. Now's my chance. I don't have to go back. I don't have to be part of all that crazy. I can start again. I can leave.

Leave Mom. Leave Sam. Leave Ford.

I shove the tears back. I don't want to leave my brother. Not with her. Not with him.

I'd have to leave my friends too. I'd have to change schools. Move away to Oklahoma. I don't want to live there. I don't want to live with my dad. I don't think he really wants me there either. Those cold, distant eyes. The way he looks at me like a stranger.

But I can't stay here either.

At Silver Lane, I hesitate. Turn left toward the highway, or right toward the neighborhood behind ours? Alison lives back there. Maybe . . . maybe she'll know what to do. I don't know. Will she help? I sit with her at lunch. That makes us friends. I can talk to her, right? Maybe her mom will know what to do.

I don't know what to do. But I can't just stand here.

I'm boiling inside, but at the same time, I'm already cooling. The January wind blows, and I ran outside without a jacket. I'm wearing shoes, sweat bottoms, and a T-shirt. That's it. I wrap my arms around myself as I walk. The sky is overcast with heavy gray clouds. As if the sky might fall on me. Crush me beneath its weight.

Crush me for real. The way I feel like all the stuff inside is already crushing me.

I sniffle. Try to push back all these thoughts.

I don't wanna die. But I don't wanna live like this either. I can't. I feel sick all the time. not like a cold or a flu. Like there's poison in me.

One step after the other. It seems like a frigid eternity before Beverly Drive. I've never been inside Alison's house, but we live close by. I know 'cause we ride the same bus, and I came here once, with Ethan. We didn't go inside 'cause her mom made us wait outside. But I remember the house is brick and stone on the first floor, and all burgundy wood on the second story. It's as big as one of the buildings in my complex that has four apartments. But with a big yard in the back. Alison has a big family. Three sisters, two brothers, her mom, stepdad, a couple dogs.

She showed pictures at lunch one time. I'd said, "You look happy."

She'd said, "We're Mormon."

I wasn't sure how she meant that. But I knew she was happier than me. Wasn't she? Wasn't everyone? No one I knew got hit at home like me. No one I knew got yelled at every day like me. If they did, they'd probably have someone to tell. Somewhere to go.

I don't have a safe place.

Do I?

This big ache opens up in me. Like a dark pit. Standing outside Alison's house. Like if I go up those front steps and ring the doorbell, she'll answer and she'll see me. Like, the *real* me. Like this. This pathetic, cold, bleeding boy. Maybe she'll laugh. Or worse, she'll feel sorry for me.

My finger is on the doorbell, but I can't push it. I don't want her to feel bad for me. I don't want anyone's pity.

I just want to be left alone. To grow up without bruises or scars or all this fighting all the time. I want Sam to go away and never come back. I want Mom to get better, to be happy, to have a job where she makes money, or marries a guy who really likes her and is nice to her. To me and Ford too. I want to stop feeling all these gross dark thoughts inside. I just want to be normal. I want to be like everyone else.

Shivering, I rub my hands against my arms. Leaves blow across the steps. Brown and gray, 'cause the leaves are dead. They fell off their tree, left the other leaves behind, left their family.

I don't want to be left alone, on the ground, decaying. Blowing through the wind, probably ending up in a ditch somewhere. Or the trash. Or melting into the ground all alone.

Thinking about all those leaves, alone, I feel real sick. Like I might puke again.

I don't want to throw up on Alison's doorstep, so I turn and leave. I walk all hurried across the street and flatten up against a tree, letting it shield me from the wind. The tree is so big it covers my whole body and then some. It protects me. From feeling too cold. Too alone. Like my mom does. I guess like Sam does too.

With them, I'm not alone. With them, I have a place. Even if it's not a good place. It's still a place. I have a bedroom with a bed and a blanket. And it's warm. And Ford's there.

So I start walking back. To home.

I stand outside my apartment for a long time. Can't bring myself to open the door. I'm afraid of what'll happen. Maybe Mom will start screaming again. Or start hitting. Or maybe she'll tell me I can't come back. Somehow that's worse.

When the sun starts to go down, I duck inside the apartment laundry room. The dryers blow warm air from their backsides. Almost instantly, feeling returns to the surface of my skin. At first, the heat is warm and comforting. Then it starts to burn, like a creature waking after being frozen for a hundred years. But it's just pain. I've felt worse. Holding my hands over the heat vent, sensation finally returns after a few minutes.

I peek out the door. From here, you can see in through my living-room window. I don't see anybody at first. Then I see Mom. She's cleaning.

I can't stay in the laundry room forever. I have to go back. Like folks always say about Band-Aids, it's better just to yank 'em off. If you go real slow, it's worse. Better to get it over with. But I keep waiting. Stalling.

Marisa takes my hand. She walks with me.

Inside, the vacuum cleaner is purring. When I walk inside, Mom vacuums until she sees me. She shuts it off and looks at me.

"Where have you been?" Mom says loud. But she's not screaming. Or even yelling. She's not mad, not fully. Just annoyed. "I was worried about you."

"Yeah, right."

"I was!" she snaps. This time her voice is raised.

"I'm tired of fighting," I say.

"So stop fighting with me," Mom says.

"I'm not! *You* are always mad. Not me!"

"Then why are you the one that's yelling?"

"I'm not yelling!" Except I am. I'm shivering again. But not from being cold. It's like all that poison in me warmed up too. And my whole body is aching. It makes me feel like I have to shout. So I'm shouting. Marisa tries to calm me down. She puts her hand on my back. But I shove it off. Not even she can stop the storm raging inside me, deep down where I shove all the bad stuff. "I hate this! I hate all of this!"

"You hate what?!"

Her. Sam. My dad. God, for abandoning us. This whole world. My life.

But I don't know how to say any of that.

Instead the pit opens up inside me again, and I fall in where it's dark and everything hurts. The apartment lights are all on, but it seems as dark as night and all the shadows seem alive and I feel sick again. I just want it all to go away.

I scream as loud as I can, "I wish I was dead. I wish I'd never been born!"

Mom's open palm crashes into my face. Like a car crashing into a wall. My ears ring, and my cheek feels like glass, shattered. Somehow the pain doesn't hurt so much as it jars me awake.

Then Mom throws her arms around me. I think this is some new attack. Takes almost a full minute to realize she's hugging me. "Don't say that," she whispers. Then she's crying. "Don't ever say that."

Her arms wrap around me tight. Squeezing. She's kissing my shoulder. "Take it back. And never say that again."

She grabs my face, gently for her, and makes me look her in the eyes. There's no anger there. No fury. Just concern. For a minute, she's my mom. My real mom. "Promise me. You won't say that again—ever."

"I . . ." I hate lying. My mouth can't form the words.

"Promise me."

It takes a long time to say anything. I'm trying not to cry. I want to be strong. I want to be better than this. I want this hug to mean something. Maybe it does. Maybe this is our fresh start? Maybe things will be different tomorrow. "I . . . I promise."

"That's my boy," Mom says. She hugs me again, kissing my forehead. Her tears are still on her cheeks when she laughs a little, and smiles at me. "Life is good, Rex. Try to remember that."

Marisa watches from the corner of the room. She presses her lips together, trying to smile. At me or my mom or both of us, I don't know. I don't know what Marisa is thinking. What she's feeling. Maybe because I don't know what to feel anymore either.

extra credit

Mrs. Humphrey, my English teacher, has a whole VHS collection of movies that were books first. You can borrow the adaptions, watch them, and write a paper for extra credit. I already have an A, but I want an A+. Plus, I like the movies.

After school, I walk Ford to our neighbor's place to play for two hours. At home, I slide the *Much Ado About Nothing* tape into the VCR. Press Play.

Cross-legged in the pink chair, I write character names and quotes to use in my spiral notebook. Shakespeare is hard to understand sometimes, so I have to pause and rewind. But I like the British accents. It reminds me of the BBC shows I watch on PBS.

When Sam comes home from work, I say, "Hey."

He grunts.

I keep watching the movie. Maybe forty-five minutes left.

Sam looks around the kitchen. "Y-you st-start dinner yet?"

I pause the movie. "You're home early. I don't start cooking until six thirty." A hard-learned lesson. 'Cause if dinner's cold when Sam gets home, he's pissed. And if I'm still making it, he's pissed.

Under his breath, he sneers, "Lazy w-wetback."

He walks down the hallway to the bathroom. With his back turned, I flip him off. Whispering to myself, "Asshole."

I continue on with the movie.

Sam showers. Gets dressed. He stares into the fridge for a long time, casting his face in gold light. He takes a beer, drinks it down. He crushes the can. Belches. Takes another, and walks into the living room. "G-g-get up."

My eyes roll. The constant struggle over who gets the comfortable chair closest to the TV. This is the only VCR in the house, or I'd move. Instead, I give up the chair. I sit on the floor.

Sam squints at the TV, scowling, like he's watching accountants do taxes. "Wh-what is this sh-shit?"

"Shakespeare. I'm watching for school."

He leans forward in the chair, watching the wedding when Claudio denounces Hero. She faints.

"G-g-gimme the remote."

"Why?"

"G-g-gimme the f-fucking remote."

I ask, "Are you going to change it?"

He makes a lunge for the remote. But I'm quicker. "It's almost over."

"I d-d-didn't w-work all d-day long to come h-home and watch s-some stupid movie in F-f-french."

"French? No. It's in old English."

He stares at me, but listens to the TV.

"That a-ain't English. Now g-g-gimme the g-goddamn

remote—" He reaches for me, but I scurry back. This pisses him off. He stomps at me, seizing my wrist, pressing.

"It *is* English!" I shout. "I'm watching this for English class."

He yanks the remote from my hand. With his other hand, he raises it up, like he'll strike. I put my hands up in a shield.

He laughs.

"F-fag af-fraid o-of his o-own shadow." Satisfied, he saunters back to the chair, sits, changes the channel. "Now, get in the kitchen."

My body is swimming with adrenaline. I feel so strong I could fly. Like I can challenge Zeus himself. I feel brave. "I'm not cooking shit for you."

"W-what'd y-you say?"

"You heard me. Cook your own dinner. I'm not your slave."

Sam's eyes light up. Shock and fury.

He walks over, a vein straining in his forehead. He says, "G-g-get up," again. So I stand.

I'm five-foot-five, a hundred and ten pounds of boy. He's six-four, well over two hundred. He blocks the light from the dining room, like a giant in front of the sun. He stabs his fingers into my chest. "Th-think you're a b-big man? Th-think you c-can t-take me? Go on. I-I-I'll g-give you the first shot."

My hands squeeze into fists. I want to. I want to hit him. But I know it'd be like a gnat hitting a mountain. Then the mountain leaping on top of the insect, crushing out the life.

"M-mouthing o-off to me? I-in m-my house? I w-work h-hard all day. P-pay the b-bills. Th-then I c-come home, a-and h-have to put up with this shit?!" With every sentence, a jab into my chest, each jab harder until Sam shoves me into the wall. "C-come on, b-big man. You w-wanna fight m-me?"

"No," I whisper.

Sam grabs his ear. "C-come again?"

"I said no!"

"Th-that's w-what I thought," Sam sneers. He spits at me. "P-pussy."

Before I can stop it, my mouth snaps back, "At least I'm not stupid."

His hand finds the back of my neck, throws me to the floor. The carpet burns my cheek as I slide across it. Then Sam's knee is in my back. "Y-you w-will r-respect me."

"No, I won't."

Facedown on the carpet, knee in my spine, hand on my neck. Pinned. Sam's other hand grabs at my right arm. I wave it, not giving him purchase. "G-god f-fucking dammit! Th-this is m-my house. I'm th-the man. M-me! I'll t-teach you respect—"

He catches my wrist, then pulls it back and up. My hand is somewhere in the middle of my back, being pulled up toward my shoulders.

"W-w-want m-me to br-break it?"

"No!"

"N-no what?!"

"What?"

Sam pulls my hand up further and I scream. Agony.

" 'S-sir.' Wh-when y-you s-speak to me, you c-call me sir."

The pain is excruciating. I don't care. I growl, "Make me."

He wrenches my arm up another inch. My fingertips touch the back of my neck. My shoulder is on fire, like it's being carved out with a knife. "W-want me to br-break it?"

A meek whine crawls out of my throat. "No."

"No, what?"

Even with the sweat drenching my shirt, my arm numb, glass shards clawing through my veins. I can't do it. I won't.

He is shouting in my ear, spit landing on my face. "S-say, *No, sir.* S-say it!"

But I already know, I'll never call him sir. 'Cause I don't respect him. 'Cause he beats me. 'Cause he beats my mom. 'Cause of what happened to my sister.

"S-say it, g-goddammit!"

No.

My face crushed into the carpet, the worst pain I've ever felt, 'cause my shoulder is tearing and my lungs are compressed, and I can't catch a breath with Sam on top of me, screaming—

Until the world goes silent. The pain goes away.

As if I'm sitting next to my body, watching this.

My face bright red, Sam sitting on me, screaming, demanding something he'll never get from me.

And next to me. My sister sits, cross-legged. Crying. She reaches over, her little hand taking mine. Let him do his worst. I'm not worried. Not anymore. 'Cause I know even if Sam kills me, Marisa is waiting on the other side.

I'm at peace with it.

I'm not alone.

I never have been.

My sister has always been with me.

I smile at her, then slam back into my own body as Sam shouts, "I-I'll br-break it. Th-that w-what you want?"

I say, "Go ahead."

The next day, I recall the sickening sound.

Like when you open a soda can.

Pop!

I remember Sam leaping off me. Scrambling into the kitchen, and staring back at me as I lay there. Laughing.

Refusing to cry, refusing to fight anymore, I laughed. A maniacal laugh. Like an insane person in a straightjacket in an asylum, having some wretched and silly realization that pain and laughter are both inescapable.

That's when Mom walked in. She started yelling, asking what happened. But I couldn't talk. I couldn't stop laughing. Until I was gasping for breath. Hyperventilating. She helped me to sit up, my right arm hanging down my side. Limp, like a dead fish.

She screamed, slapped Sam. He sat there on the linoleum, covering himself with his arms, letting her shower him with hits. The giant was reduced to a ball as Mom shrieked and kicked.

My sister sat with me, telling me to breathe, trying to smile, trying to say it would be all right. But her tears made her words unconvincing.

I remember Mom helping me up. Dazed and confused. Maybe from the pain. Or the lack of oxygen. And we stumbled outside. It was so dark, except for the glow of the pool. Aquamarine radiating up into the night, bugs flying over it, wondering if the light was heaven or if it was death. The cool air of night felt crisp on my skin.

Our neighbor, a nurse, asked what happened. Mom said I fell down the stairs. Even though we live on the first floor. Mom said I shouldn't be horsing around. Even as she lied, her eyes were full of apologies.

"It's not broken, just dislocated," the nurse said.

She helped shove my arm back to where it should be. Said to put ice on it. To go to the doctor immediately. My mom lied again, saying we would. But we don't have insurance. We don't have money for that. And for once, Mom couldn't know if I would tell the truth or not.

why

She is sitting at the table, staring at it.

I put down my backpack, and say, "Mom?"

Her eye is swollen and purple. Her lip bloody.

I want to punch Sam. I want to hit him. Hurt him. The way he does us. No, I want to hurt him worse. I want to take a baseball bat to his fingers, breaking every bone in them, so he can't hit us anymore. Hit him until he can't hurt anyone, until he's—

Marisa is in the corner of my mind, shaking her head, *No*.

Shoving the anger back, into the back-back of my mind, cramming it into the darkness with everything else. There's no room, but I shove it anyways. My skin crawling with anger, like fire ants just under my skin. Rage.

In the kitchen, I fill a sandwich bag with ice cubes. I sit next to Mom. I put it up to her lip.

She recoils, surprised. "When did you get home?"

"Just now." I offer her the bag of ice. She takes it. "For your eye."

We sit in silence for a long time.

I can't help it. I ask what I always ask. "Why?"

"Why what?"

"Why do you stay with him?"

For once, she doesn't explode. She doesn't cry. She doesn't lash out. She just shakes her head.

"Life is a struggle, Rex. To wake up, to go to work, to find love, to raise a family. Everything is hard."

"He makes it harder."

Mom shakes her head again.

"I watched a show on TV the other night. There's places we can go. Shelters. We can leave. We can start over. We can—"

Mom laughs. It's not joyous. It's not sarcastic. Just a dry "Ha." She changes the hand holding the ice pack. She flexes her cold fingers. "On TV, in the movies, they make everything seem like a workable situation. But in the real world, when you work yourself to the bone, just to put food in your mouth and keep the lights on—you don't have a choice to just leave."

"We have my dad's child-support check."

Mom rolls her eyes. "Two hundred dollars doesn't even cover rent."

"We can go to Abuela's."

"I am *not* living with my mother."

"It's better than this! Living in fear, waiting for him to punch one of us."

"He only gets angry when we upset him."

"You're defending him."

"I am not."

"You are! You think this is OK?" I point at her face. "Do you? Do you think you deserve this?"

This time, she doesn't shake her head.

refund

get the mail. Usually it's just bills and junk mail. But today one of the envelopes is light brown, almost orange. In the window is Mom's name and address with a background of yellow fading into green. It's a check.

All at once, my head is swirling with a plan.

I run inside our apartment, checking all the rooms.

"What are you doing?" Mom asks.

"Is Sam here?"

"No, he's still at work. Why?"

I hold up the bright envelope. "It's your tax refund. We can leave."

Mom studies my face, like I'm telling a joke she doesn't get. "And go where? We can't afford a vacation."

"No. I mean we can leave—" I stop myself 'cause Ford is watching us. "Watch your cartoons. Mom and I are just talking." I pull Mom into her bedroom and close the door. "You want to leave. I know you do. So do I. So let's take Ford and just go. The three of us. The money from this check will help us start over. We can pack everything tomorrow while he's at work, and just go. Or I guess, maybe we need a few days, to find a new apartment, and put down a deposit and—"

"Stop," Mom says. She sits on her bed. "Just stop."

"What? Why? Do you have a better plan?"

"We can't—" She clucks her tongue. Then sighs. "We can't just leave Sam."

"Why not?"

"He's Ford's dad."

"Yeah, well, he can settle visitation rights *after* we go."

"Rex, stop."

She glares at me, like she's the pope and I'm blaspheming. Like I've somehow offended her. "I don't like hearing you talk like this."

"Like what? Wanting to change our lives for the better?"

Her head falls into her hands.

I ask, "Aren't you tired?"

In a low whisper, "Yes."

I sit down next to her. I take one of her hands. "So let's do this. Let's go."

When she looks up, her eyes are all conflict. "Let me—just let me think about it."

"What's to think about?" I snap, trying not to yell.

Mom looks out of her window. The sunlight beams in, lighting her face. "We might have to get a smaller apartment."

"Fine! I'll sleep in the living room. You and Ford can have the room."

A hint of a smile pulls at the corner of her mouth. "There's that new complex off the highway. It's walking distance from your school. It wouldn't hurt to look at them."

"For real?"

"Tell you what. I'll pick you up from school on Friday. We'll go look . . . just look, OK? But Sam *can't* know."

I throw myself at Mom, hugging her.

This weight leaves my chest. Like I can breathe a little deeper.

I am sitting outside of my school. Class let out at three. It's almost four now. With everyone gone, the parking lot empty, the place feels strange. A ghost of itself.

Mom's car is nowhere in sight. I wonder if she looked at the apartments without me. Or if she forgot. Or if she had a car accident. I'm equal parts pissed and worried.

At the pay phone, I press "0" to make a collect call. But no one answers.

At four thirty, I'm sick of waiting. I start the walk home.

It takes an hour and a half, walking on the shoulder of the highway, to get home. The sun is getting close to the horizon behind me. As I walk down Cattle Drive, I hear a motorcycle gunning its engine in the distance. *Vroom-vroom.*

In my apartment parking lot, a streak of red jets down to the other end, swerves, and returns—slowing just outside my apartment. The driver pulls up in front of Mom and Ford, clapping. Before he takes off his helmet, I already know it's Sam. What I don't know, is how he got a new motorcycle. We can't afford it. We don't have the extra—

Then it clicks.

My two-day-old dream dies, and something collapses inside my chest. Not an organ, but some little light. Like a candle being blown out.

When Sam sees me, he lifts up the black visor. He's beaming with pride. "R-r-rex, you w-want a ride on my new b-bike?"

Without an answer, I pass Sam. My eyes glued to my mom's face. She doesn't turn away. She doesn't look down. There's no remorse in her face. No apology on her lips. Her eyes meet mine head-on. Like two cars driving toward each other as fast as they can, daring the other to swerve off. But neither of us will. In this situation, there will be no winner.

She says, "Rex—"

My insides are boiling. My fists squeeze so hard they could turn coal to diamonds. All of me is furious . . . desperate, wanting to punch something. Or someone.

"Wait, Rex, let me explain—"

If I stop now, I will do something terrible.

So I keep walking. I pass doing nothing. Except saying, "Mom—fuck you."

night

I can't sleep. I toss and turn. Right side. Left side. Back to my right side.

I'm angry all the time. I try not to talk to Mom. When I do, it comes out in sneers and growls. Then she growls back, or pinches me, or slaps me, trying to remind me she's still my mother.

Hours of tossing in my sheets. Finally, I turn onto my back and stare straight up at the bottom of the bunk bed. The wood frame reminds me of a coffin. I remind myself that just inches above, Ford is sleeping, hopefully dreaming happy dreams.

I lie there, waiting. This shudder rolls through me, a wave of anxiety, of dread and anticipation. Waiting for what? Maybe for arguing to sound outside the room. But it doesn't. Tonight, it's quiet.

Absent.

Like something is missing.

Without the screaming, it's lonely. I feel a million miles away from civilization. My heart starts to race.

My body tenses up. I feel in danger. Like I can't breathe. I want to run and cry and scream. But I just lie there. Shivering despite the blankets. Shaking, as if I'm staring down a rattlesnake. Like I might die. Like I am dying.

Then Marisa is there, a soft blue glow in the room. She crawls up the bed in her pajamas, and lies across from me. Her head on the same pillow. Her eyes—so like Ford's—meet mine. She says, *Breathe.*

It's like I forget sometimes. Until she reminds me.

Without a word, she reminds me of stars, twinkling at night. Of warm summer days at the pool, sun shining. Reminds me of school hallways. Of my friends. Laughter at lunchtime. Phone calls when we whisper well after bedtime. She reminds me of my favorite songs on the radio. Of skateboarding with Todd. Of camping with Liam. Of playing Nintendo with neighbors. Of talking comic books with Ethan. Of the X-Men. Those bright-colored pages, of vibrant yellows and blues and reds, adventures across the stars, pain given purpose. Marisa reminds me of Ford, his laughter, building LEGO sets with him, the way he dances, copying every move he sees on the TV and replicating it, only smaller.

My sister reminds me of visits to Abuela's. Trips to the Abilene Mall, or the Dyess Air Force Base, or just to Walmart, where my grandmother lets me roam the toy section without judgment. Or to bookstores, with the fresh smell of pages with words, or libraries, the same smell, only older. Or books, where I read and lose myself in the fiction of other worlds or space or the past. Of trips to the movies, when I go alone to the matinee and disappear inside the screen for two hours.

She reminds me of the cat, the one we don't own but that we feed from time to time. And in return, he drops off dead mice on our doorstep, then prances inside, rubbing against our legs, purring as he crawls into my lap. Reminds me of riding my bike to the edge of the lake, where I pick grass, noticing nothing but the blue sky reflected in the gentle curls of the water, lapping at the edge.

My sister keeps reminding me of the little things in life, the ones that make me smile. She does this without saying a word, except sometimes, to giggle, when I think up something silly, like the way a rabbit's nose twitches, as my mind slowly drifts off to sleep.

houston

Our car pulls up to a brown-and-tan house. It has a two-car garage, but the driveway is full. The other cars are newer and nicer than ours. Mom snaps at Sam, "I thought this was a family function. Just your brothers, wives, and kids?"

"I-i-it's a b-barbecue."

"I have to peeeeeee!" Ford squeals. He pounds the back of Mom's seat with his little fists. He's half my size, but feels just as cramped in the backseat after a four-hour drive.

The door opens, blasting us with Houston heat. The air heavy and sticky.

From the front door, Sam's brother Gary shouts, "You made it!!" Gary is followed by his wife, Sarah.

Sarah wears a flower dress, golden earrings, and lipstick. She beams at me and Ford like the sun, hugging us. "Rex, look how you've grown. We haven't seen you since, when? When y'all were living with us in Paris, Texas?"

"That was fourth grade," I say. "So . . . six years ago?"

After he hugs Sam, Gary shakes my hand. He pretends that I break his. "Look at that grip! You're practically a man. Wanna beer? Ha! Just kidding."

"Come on. Party's back here." Sarah waves for us to follow. "Your cousins can't wait to see you, Ford. This is the first time you'll meet Dennis's sons, huh?"

In the backyard, there are almost twenty people. Adults drinking beer, chatting. A few crowding a table of food while others chat around a sizzling grill. Kids run around, playing tag. Two dogs sit under the shade of a tree, panting.

I'm following Ford when Mom yanks me back, hissing, "Stay next to me."

"Why?"

"We're in enemy territory."

I pull my arm back. "This is Sam's family."

"They're thick as thieves," she says. "You'll see. You and I aren't welcome."

I think of my own dad's family. How they never call. How they watch me when I visit, recoil at the mention of my mother. How her photo has been removed from every single family album in their homes.

My mom is like a plague that no one wants to catch. Better to keep your distance.

I understand why from my dad's family. But not Sam's. How can she cause trouble when we never seen them? I've never even met Sam's other two brothers.

Gary walks Sam up to two men. All of them tower over six feet, have blond hair and blue eyes. Sam says, "D-D-Dennis. K-K-Kent."

The three big brothers huddle around Sam. The hug lasts

for a while. Even though Dennis is the biggest, he has tears in his eyes. Kent says, "Good to see ya, runt."

They're all smiling and sniffling. I wonder why they don't talk, why they don't see each other.

I can't imagine not seeing Ford every day. He annoys me, but he's my brother.

Sam picks up Ford, introducing him. His brothers say hi. With the cousins at their feet, the whole family is glowing. Happy. I want that too. But when Sam points over to me and Mom, all that joy goes out of the men's eyes.

Gary grits his teeth and walks Ford and the cousins over to the swing set. Kent goes to get another beer. Only Dennis walks over. A gold cross on a gold string dangles around his neck.

"Luciana," he says, his voice chilly despite the heat.

"Dennis," Mom says.

I wave. "Hi. I'm Ford's brother, Rex."

Dennis shakes my hand. "Nice to meet you. I've heard good things."

"From who?"

He chuckles. "Have you had anything to eat yet? Go help yourself."

I don't hesitate. The long folding table is loaded with potato chips and French onion dip, tortilla chips and salsa, grilled hot dogs, onions, relish, buns, mustard and ketchup. I ignore the veggie tray, skipping straight to the Chips Ahoy chocolate-chip cookies.

Dennis said I could use the hammock on the side of the house if I wanted, so I do. Hours go by, Ford running around with his cousins, adults talking among themselves. Every once in a while, I look up, and see Mom standing in the corner, alone. Staring.

I ignore her. I'm halfway through Stephen King's *Dark Tower: The Gunslinger*, and it's getting really good. The sun heads down, and guests file out. The adults and kids head inside. I hear a football game on through the window. It's still light enough to read, so I stay in the hammock—until I hear the scream.

I'm out of the hammock and running, 'cause I'd know that voice anywhere: Ford.

The backyard is empty, except Ford, kicking and screaming, being dragged by his hair by the two dogs. Before I can get there, a neighbor is leaping over the fence. He kicks one dog, and slaps the other away. While he wards off one, the second snaps again, gnashing his teeth, clamping down on Ford's hair. I pin my body on top of the dog, shoving my hands into its mouth, wrenching for its jaw to open.

Then I'm on my knees, holding Ford in my arms as he cries. Tears run down his cheeks. The neighbor is guarding us, shouting at Dennis's porch door.

I check my brother. There's no blood. Just some missing hair. Relief washes over me. The dogs linger, watching Ford, like he's a squirrel in my arms. Growling rumbles in their throats. "*Shhhh*," I say. "It's OK."

Then everyone is shouting. Dennis at his neighbor. Gary to Sarah to keep their kids back. One of the dogs launches at me, but Sam yanks Ford from my arms, holding him out of the dog's reach. Dennis grabs the dog by its collar, jerking so hard I wince. He holds the dog two feet off the ground, choking it until it whimpers. He kicks the other dog in its side.

I shout, "Hey! Stop it!"

Dennis shoots me this dark stare. I know it well, 'cause Sam's given it to me a hundred times. The look says, *Stay out of this.*

Dennis is dragging both dogs by their choke collars, even as they whine and cry, across the yard. He throws them into a cage. He muzzles them. Then locks the door.

My heart is beating in my ear. My whole body hot and cold, powerful, like I could run a race, or maybe puke. I'm so dizzy with the heartbeat, I hadn't heard Mom until now. She's screaming at family, "*That monster needs to be put down. Did you see? Did all of you see? That beast tried to murder my son!*"

Ford is crying in Sam's arms. Gary puts his hand gently on Sarah's arm, guiding her and their children back inside. Kent is on the porch, drinking a beer, glaring at my mother. Dennis is walking back, fury in his eyes.

It does feel like enemy territory here, I realize. My mom and I aren't wanted. I say, "Mom, stop." I get in front of her, try to lock her eyes with mine. "Ford's OK. Let it go."

Spit flies from her mouth, screaming, "*He's not OK! Look at him!*"

"He's scared. Your shouting is making it worse."

"*I'm* not making it worse!" she shrieks. "*I'm* not the one hosting a party with two killer animals walking around."

"Ford must have done something—" Dennis starts.

"Then. *Lock. Them. Up!*" Mom claps her hands after each word. "*How stupid are you? I should sue! I'll sue everyone here. I'll take you for every dime you have. I'll have those beasts put down!*"

"L-l-luciana," Sam stutters, angry veins showing in his forehead.

"Why aren't you on my side?!" she screams. "They tried to kill your son."

She starts shoving Sam. She starts slapping at him. One

arm holds Ford; with the other, he tries to grab her flying hands. I have to step between them and shout in her face, "Mom, stop!"

Everyone stares. Sam. His family. The neighbor. The dogs in their cage. I wish I could muzzle my mom. Why can't she stop herself? Why can't I stop her?

She's shouting around me. At the top of her lungs, making a scene. On the porch, Kent with his beer says, "What are you gonna do? Send Sam back to jail?"

Then silence from everyone. Even my mom.

Then it becomes clear to me. They know. They all know about him in jail. But what about Marisa? Do they know what happened? 'Cause I still don't.

"What'd you say?!" Mom snaps, starting for Kent.

I step in the way. "Mom, enough. Stop. It's over. Everyone is OK."

"*I'm* not OK! *Ford's* not OK!"

"*So comfort him!*" I point at my brother. "*Stop worrying about everyone else and take care of your son!*"

I don't realize how loud I'm shouting until I stop. I had to out-shout her. Now everyone is staring at me.

A cold sweat floods over me. The hot dogs and chips and onion dip and four cups of soda churn in my stomach.

Mom remembers herself. Remembers Ford. She hugs him, whispering. "It's OK. Everything's going to be OK."

I think, *Except that it's not.*

Mom and Sam argue in the front yard, shouting. It's been almost two hours. Every few minutes she takes a swing, but he lets it happen. I don't know if Sam would hit Mom in front of his family.

It doesn't help that when Kent gets in his truck to leave, he rolls down the window and shouts, "Bitch!" She picks up a garden rock to throw it. Sam grabs her arm in time, so it misses—though only barely.

Dennis, his wife, their two sons; Gary, Sarah, their two kids; Ford and me. We're all inside, pretending we can't hear. But we all can. That's why I'm distracting the kids. Cartoons on the TV, and a building contest with LEGO bricks. The adults are at the dining table with a puzzle, whispering.

"Rex. Would you come here a second?" Dennis asks.

I walk over.

"Is she always like this?"

I nod.

"You know that kind of behavior isn't normal, right?"

"It's not just her," I mutter.

"No one is perfect," Dennis says, "not Sam, not me, no one."

I stand there. Not knowing what to say. I know on some level Mom isn't well. But it pisses me off that Dennis is saying it. I don't think a few hours with my mom gives him any right to judge her. What does he know?

"You did good today," Gary says, pulling me aside. "You handled yourself really well. You handled your mom really well."

"It didn't help."

"But you tried," Gary says. "And you saved your brother."

"Nah. The neighbor did that."

"You don't give yourself enough credit. You're a hero."

I kinda do this nervous laugh. 'Cause I think he's being sarcastic. Then I realize he's serious. I think of my comics, of the X-Men. Of superheroes saving the planet. I shake my head. "I'm no hero."

"You are," Sarah says. "Look at your hands."

They're all covered in red lines, scratches and scabs and Band-Aids. With my mom making a scene earlier, I hadn't even noticed they were covered in blood until Sarah took me inside, into the bathroom, and poured hydrogen peroxide on them.

"They're just scratches."

Sarah gives me this look like she isn't going to argue. Instead, she just hugs me real hard. In my ear, she whispers, "You're a good person."

It's like she strikes me. 'Cause I don't believe that. Not for a second. If I were a good person, this wouldn't be my life. If I were a good person, God wouldn't let me live like this. I'd have a two-story house and parents who love me and can pay the bills and never fight, and my sister would be alive.

Good people have happy families.

They don't have . . . whatever *this* is.

Outside, Mom gets louder. Shouting that Sam is a loser, has always been a loser, will always be a loser.

I think, *We're all losers here. None of us is winning any prizes.*

I turn up the TV so the kids can't hear. Then I walk to the door.

Mom is swinging. Not open-palmed slaps. Her fists.

That's when Dennis storms past me and shouts, "Get off my lawn. You're not welcome here. Sam and the boys can stay. But you have to go. Now."

Mom is shoving at Sam and Dennis, trying to get past them. They won't let her. "I'm uninvited? Fine. Let me get my son.

Rex! Rex, come here. We're leaving. You and me. We don't need these assholes. Let's go."

My voice trembles when I say, "No."

"Rex. Get over here. Now."

"No. I'm staying."

"Rex! This isn't funny."

"I agree. It's not funny."

"Get over here now! Or else!"

"Or else what? You had your chance to leave. You chose to stay. That was your choice. This is mine."

"To stay with Sam?!" she seethes.

"No. To stay with Ford."

"Rex!" she screams. Less out of anger and more out of hurt.

Now I can't look at her. So I look down.

Dennis is pointing down the street. "Leave, Luciana."

She leaps at Sam, ripping the keys from his hands. She gets in the car. Slams the door. Guns the ignition, still in park. Her eyes find me—

Like I've hurt her the worst . . .

Worse than Sam . . .

Worse than my father . . .

Worse than anyone that came before . . .

She stares at me. 'Cause I'm the monster here.

Then she drives away.

I can't stop seeing her eyes.

The hurt in them.

The pain.

All through dinner with Sam's family, I keep thinking about it. I wonder where she is. What she's eating for dinner. I imagine her eating alone at a counter in a dark diner. And she's crying. 'Cause she's alone in a strange place. And her family made her leave. And her son wouldn't go with her.

I could have.

I could have gone.

I could have taken her side. Or gotten in the car when she asked. Or chased her car down the street until she stopped and let me go with her.

But I didn't want to. I didn't want to stay with Sam, but I didn't want to go with my mom either.

I'm so tired. Of all of it.

I wanted her to go.

And now I feel sick thinking about all of it. About her eating alone. Going to a dim motel, sleeping alone in a musty room with scratchy blankets and a flickering neon light outside the window. What if something bad happens? What if she's robbed? What if she's murdered? What if she's so mad, she didn't stop to eat? What if she left town. What if she took the car and kept driving. What if she has an accident? What if she kills herself?

I leave the dinner table—where everyone is talking and laughing and Ford is eating mac-n-cheese-n-bacon with the biggest smile, and Sam has this warmness in his eyes I haven't seen in forever, like he couldn't hurt a fly, let alone his stepson—and I go to the bathroom and I throw up into the toilet.

Twice.

Maybe 'cause I'm feeling two things at once.

One—I'm worried about Mom.

And two—part of me hopes she never comes back. 'Cause maybe then . . . maybe life would be a little bit easier.

And for once, I want easy.

It's evil and I know it's evil. But that's 'cause *I* am evil. Mom is right. She's always been right. A good son would have gone with her. He would protect her. He would never let Sam hit her. He wouldn't have left that summer, and his sister would be alive.

My sister died 'cause I'm not good. It was my fault and I'm a bad person and I deserve bad things to happen to me 'cause I am evil. God hates me. I was born this way, wicked, full of vile thoughts and dark instincts. I can't stop them, I can't shut them out. And no matter how often I try to do right, I fail again and again.

'Cause I'm not the hero.

I'm the monster.

Dennis takes all of us to the zoo. Ford gets his face painted like a tiger. On the way home, we stop for gas. Sam buys me a Mexican jumping bean in a clear plastic box. When I hold it, it jumps in my hand, like its alive. I don't know how it works, if it's alive or dead. If its dead, then how does it move? Then I wonder how I kept moving today, even though I feel dead inside. 'Cause all I can see is Mom staring at me with her eyes full of pain.

Later Sam, his brothers, their families, we're all watching a movie together. In our pajamas. The adults are on the couches, giggling. The kids on the floor on a pallet of blankets and pillows. Off to the side, I get a big recliner chair all to myself. We watch Disney's *The Sword in the Stone*.

The whole time, I'm thinking Arthur is lucky, 'cause he's an orphan. Plus he has this destiny to be a hero. He's good. He doesn't wish bad things on people. Heroes don't do that.

After the movie, everyone says good night. Hugs are exchanged. Moms kiss their children, tucking them in. I don't recall Mom ever tucking me in. Then I punish myself for thinking that, 'cause I don't know where she is. If she's alive or dead. I feel like I don't know anything more about her than I do my jumping bean, except that she lost a snow globe when she was little.

Gary and Sarah and their kids sleep in the guest room. Dennis's wife tucks her boys into their beds, and Ford joins them in a sleeping bag on the floor. Sam makes up the couch, and I get the pallet. Under the blankets, I start to drift off, half-dreaming of my mom in a plastic box in my pocket, but not jumping at all. Still.

Hushed voices wake me. In the kitchen, Sam and Dennis are whispering.

"Here. I want to give you this."

"A B-b-bible? W-why?"

"I believe you need it in your life now, more than ever."

"I a-a-already b-believe in God."

"But do you live your life by His ways?"

There's this long silence that hangs in the air.

Sam says, "R-r-rex, y-y-you awake?"

I don't say anything. I don't move. I keep my eyes closed.

Someone sniffles. Then I hear Sam crying.

"I-I-I d-don't w-want to . . ."

"You don't want to what?"

"H-h-hit h-her."

"But you do."

"Y-y-yeah."

"Are you drinking?"

"Y-y-yeah."

"So you've become Luther. You've become our father?"

"D-d-dennis, d-don't . . ."

"Say it. You've become Dad."

Sam weeps.

"Don't paint a pretty picture in your head, Sam. Dad was a bastard. He'd get drunk, what? Two, three, four nights a week? He'd come home, slamming doors. Come in our room, shake us awake, ask where Mom was. She'd be asleep in bed, but he was too drunk to find his own room—"

"I-I-I'm n-not h-him . . ."

"Then we'd hear her. Hear the slaps. Mom's cries. He was violent, Sam. With her, *and* with us. You don't want to be like that."

"I d-don't."

"You hit Ford?"

"N-never."

"You hit Rex?"

Sam is crying again. Slow quiet sobs.

"I-it's n-not my fault. She d-drives me to it. L-luciana m-makes me."

"Nobody makes you do anything, little brother. God gave us free will. Jesus died for your sins. The Holy Spirit runs through our veins so that we can be better men. But you have to choose to do good. You have to make a conscious effort to be a Christian. What happened to AA? You were in the twelve-step program for how long?"

"T-two y-years."

"And then?"

"I n-n-needed a d-drink."

"You *wanted* a drink."

"N-no. I needed it."

"When was the last time you went to church?"

Silence.

"Go this Sunday. And the next. And the Sunday after. You need to find Jesus again. You need him here. In your heart. You have two boys, and they need you. Luciana can't be there for them, not in the way they need her. But you can—"

"I-I-I k-know," Sam says.

Dennis asks, "Will you pray with me?"

The two brothers ask for help. For strength. For acceptance. They ask for love and guidance. For Luciana to be made better. For Sam to be stronger, for him to not lay hands on her. For the Good Lord to come into our house, and protect us from evil.

The prayer lasts a long time.

So long, I start to fall asleep.

On the edge of dreaming, I wonder if God is listening. I wonder if he'll help. If he'll hear Sam's prayers. 'Cause I've prayed. I've prayed so many times I've lost count. And he's never answered. He's never helped me.

But maybe that's 'cause I'm evil.

traitor

When we get home, Mom isn't there. She's been home, but she's left again. I feel sick to my stomach.

The rest of the night, Ford keeps asking, "Where's Mom?"

I answer honestly. "I don't know."

In my bunk bed, I stare at the wood above me. Seeing things in the flesh of the surface. The wooden waves become faces. Demons. Eyes judging me.

I don't sleep, but I'm not awake either.

Sometime in the middle of the dark stretch of night, I hear the front door open. Then close.

Keys jangle, dropped, landing on the carpet.

Padded footsteps. Two, three, four. Then my bedroom door swings open.

Her hair stringy and wild, like a bird's nest on the side of her head. She wears the same clothes as the last time I saw her, her face grimy. She smells like she hasn't showered in days.

Mom stands there, vacancy in her eyes. 'Til she sees me.

Her brows arch down. Angry or appalled, I can't tell. But in the dark room, her eyes look black. Possessed by hate.

She doesn't move, as if turned to stone.

The room is filled with quiet, as if we're underwater. Until she whispers, so low I barely catch it.

"My son," she says. "Judas."

"I didn't betray you."

"Liar," she spits.

I want to cave. I want to run to her, hug her, fall on my knees, beg her to forgive me so she'll love me again, so she'll be my mommy. But I've done that a hundred times. She hasn't forgiven me. She'll never forgive me. I don't blame her. I haven't forgiven me either.

"You did it to hurt me," she said.

"No, I didn't."

She says, "You chose him over me."

I want to scream, *You've always chosen him over* me*!* But I don't.

Instead, I say, "No, I didn't."

She doesn't move. Doesn't say anything. Her gaze shifts into a glare, stabbing at me, trying to demolish me the way it used to. As if I hadn't heard her, as if she didn't hear me, she says again, "You chose *him.* Over *me.*"

"No," I repeat, "I didn't."

"You didn't come when I needed. You left me alone. You chose Sam over me."

"I didn't choose him," I say. "I just didn't choose you."

I feel Marisa's hand squeeze mine. Letting me know it's OK. So I say it.

"I chose me."

eggs

Saturday morning, Ford wakes up before I do. He's watching *Power Rangers*. I think it's about the stupidest show ever, but I still watch it. I even know all the names and colors of the rangers, and their dinosaurs.

On a commercial break, I pour two bowls of Cheerios from the yellow box. I add whole milk, then sprinkle each with a spoonful of sugar.

"Two spoons of sugar!" Ford says.

"One is plenty," I say.

"Twooooooo!" He leans over the arm of the pink chair and slides to the floor like a blob. "Please. I need two."

He makes me laugh, so I give him a second. I add a second to mine too.

We eat cereal while we watch *Teenage Mutant Ninja Turtles*. I'm a little old for kids' stuff, but I really like *TMNT*. I have a few of the action figures, under my bed. After *TMNT* is what I've been waiting for all morning: *X-Men*. The animated series isn't as good as the comics, but it's still cool to see them come to life on TV.

Especially with Sam still sleeping, and Mom gone at the store. Ford and I get to watch Wolverine and Cyclops and Storm and even stupid Jubilee, without Mom talking loud over it. Of course, as soon as it starts, Mom opens the front door with her knee. Car keys dangle from her finger while she juggles four grocery bags.

"Good morning, good morning, good morning!" She's all cheerful. Smiling. It makes me cringe. Her mood's like a swing, going back and forth, back and forth, only you never know when it'll speed up or stop, 'cause no one is in the swing.

She's wearing sweat-bottom cut-offs and an old T-shirt. A little ponytail on top of her head bobs this way and that. Smiling ear to ear, she sings, "I got you a surprise."

"For me?" Ford asks, forgetting the cartoon. "What is it?"

Mom says, "It's for the whole family."

I think of fishing, how you use worms to bait the hook. I want a surprise, too, but only if it's good. Sometimes, especially in our house, surprises go bad. I keep watching *X-Men*, until Mom says, "Rex, aren't you curious?"

Carefully, I say, "Sure."

She unloads the bags onto the kitchen counter. With delicate care, Mom pulls a clear plastic container from the grocery bag. Inside are four small fist-sized eggs. Each has pastel frosting, each with a name, written in cursive icing: *Mom*, *Sam*, *Ford*, and *Rex*.

"Is that cake?" I ask, my mouth watering.

Mom nods yes. "Easter is next week. And I saw these, and—"

"Yes!" Ford says.

He reaches for the cakes at the same time our Mom moves forward. Like two cars, they collide.

The plastic bottom falls out, and gravity snatches the four cakes. I dive to catch them, but too late. All four smash onto the kitchen floor.

All the joy, all the excitement and pride, drains away from my mom's face—like the world is punishing her for a good deed. Her bottom jaw quivers, like a tremor before an earthquake.

"It's OK," I say gently. "Look, only mine and yours got messed-up. Our names are just a little smudged—"

In a whisper, Mom says, "Everything is ruined."

As if she'd been holding up the world, her legs shake, then give out. The weight is just too much. Her knees and palms crash to the linoleum. On all fours, she peers over the cakes—like they were something more important, like they were alive.

The pink frosting reminds me of my sister.

Maybe it does Mom too. 'Cause tears stream down her cheek. She reaches out in slow motion, pauses, then touches the edge of the cake softly. Like she's caressing the cheek of a sleeping baby.

I stare at her finger, the delicate touch, the heft of the air around her. I wonder if she's seeing my sister. If this is how she reached out to her stillborn child—

Afraid.

Upset.

Alone.

Her eyes glisten, the tears catching sun from the windows.

I try to talk but a knot chokes my throat, my own eyes welling up. I manage to say, "Mom, it's OK. It's just cake."

Struggling, she says, "It's not OK. It'll never be OK."

Then she's shouting, "I try to do one nice thing. *One!* Just one little thing, a gift for my family, but no! God won't let me have even that!"

Gently, slowly, I guide Ford behind me. The grenade's pin fell out, but maybe I can put it back in.

"Let's go back to the store. We'll get new ones."

"We can't!" she roars. "I work and I work and I work, until I hurt. Until my bones hurt. For what? Nickels and dimes! I want to do one nice thing for my family, and this happens. *This!* I always come short."

"Mom, it's OK. These floors are spotless. You cleaned them yesterday. I'll eat mine, I don't care—"

"No!" she shouts. "No, no, no, *no!*"

She slams her fists against the cakes, smashing them into mulch. Again and again. I try to stop her, to reach out. *"Don't touch me! Everything I touch turns to shit!!"*

She cries for a long time after, while I stare at the pink frosting. Ford watches too. So does Marisa. My little brother and sister watch me wondering: What if I had just stayed with Mom that summer?

Then Marisa would be here, the five of us eating cake.

But Marisa shakes her head. *You didn't know. No one told you. You were just a kid.*

For the first time, I wish I could share my sister with Mom. Maybe Mom wouldn't be so upset if she knew Marisa was still here, trying to help.

door

The screaming reminds me of a hill. It gets louder and louder, the way a hill gets higher and higher. When the hill starts to reach its point, when the shouting reaches a certain level, the fall comes next. Everything is downhill after.

Ford looks at me, his eyes big, wet with tears. I say, "Don't listen." As if that were possible.

Sam's bass. Mom's shrill. They find their way through the apartment walls like water through sand on the beach.

"Hop on my bed."

"Yours?" Ford confirms. 'Cause I never let him in my bed. It's my space. But I nod. He hops onto my bed, the bunk beneath his. I tuck Abuela's quilt into the top beams, creating a cave. From under my bed, I get out my little TV, the one Aunt Lora gave me. It's the size of an adult shoebox, with a screen the size of a baseball card. I turn the knob until a black-and-white image appears. I tune to a channel with cartoons. I plug in the headphones, carefully putting them over Ford's ears.

Now he doesn't have to hear. He doesn't have to see.

I try to ignore them.

Maybe they'll stop.

I open my textbooks, try to study.

Maybe they won't start hitting.

But the screaming's so loud.

Maybe they'll make up.

I shove my books away, throwing the pencil.

Maybe they'll hug.

My fists gripped so tight, I lose feeling in both hands.

Maybe they'll sit down.

I try to read comic books. To go somewhere else in my head.

Talk peacefully.

But the yells don't stop.

I ready myself to hear the thick thud of fist hitting flesh.

Mom's voice sharpens, coming in for the verbal blow that'll start the violence.

And then I'm racing to my door. To say something. To do something. Anything. To end this before it gets—

Sam shouts, "St-stop! I d-don't w-want this. J-j-just l-let me l-leave."

I walk into the living room in time to see my mom throw herself in front of the door. Her arms and legs like an X, she blocks his exit.

"M-m-move, Luciana. I don't w-want to f-fight y-you. L-let me g-go."

And Mom. *My* mom. Her eyes like a deadly snake in its nest, ready to fight for its life. Her teeth shine with spit as she hisses, "You wanna go through this door? You'll have to hit me first!"

"I n-need s-some air. M-m-move," Sam says. He reaches for the doorknob. She gnashes her teeth and claws him, trying to sink her talons in.

Ripping his arm back, her nails pull skin, drawing blood.

He makes this sucking sound as he grabs the wound in pain. "F-fucking m-move!"

I find my own voice. Shouting, "Let him leave!"

"*No!*" Mom screams back at both of us. She gnashes her teeth at Sam. "*You wanna fight? Fight me!*"

Something goes out of Sam, like a spirit out of his body. His vigor fades, he hunches, his eyes sadden. He says, "I d-don't w-want to f-fight you anymore. I'm t-t-tired."

And Mom screams, "*Hit me, goddammit!*"

And Sam whispers, "No."

Then she's in his face, slapping him, calling him worthless. A fucking bus driver. A failed swimmer. A failed lawnmower man. A failed everything. A sad excuse for a man. A faggot. Why he's too scared to hit her? She says she should go out and find a real man. A real man who can take care of her. Not him. Not Sam. Not some pussy.

And that's the top of the hill.

Sam grabs her by the hair with one hand, and slaps her as hard as he can. Then he swings. Like a boxer at a punching bag. Right in the stomach.

I wonder if this is how my sister died.

Mom slumps down to the ground, collapsing onto hands and knees. Sam opens the door, walks past her, into the real world, out where other people live, where normal life occurs. He leaves the door open.

Sunlight spills inside, falling on Mom. She looks up at me, blood dripping from lip to chin, and she smiles.

gone

hop off the school bus. I wave to Aubrey and Teddy and Kate. They go right, I go left. Inside the apartment complex, I walk along the curb. One foot in front of the other. I start counting steps, but my mind wanders forward. To my apartment. To what lies inside.

Which version of my mom?

The one who smiles and laughs and buys cookies with her tip money?

Or the other one?

I hear the wails from the parking lot. The devastation in her cries throw me back to the airport parking lot. The sound of loss.

Ford.

My feet carry me forward so fast, one of my untied shoes flies off. I leave it behind. I'm screaming, "Ford! Ford?!"

Inside the apartment, Mom is collapsed on the floor, her

face in tears. Ford sits next to her, petting her back. Just like I used to do.

Breathless, I pull him into my arms. "Are you OK? Are you hurt?"

He's confused. "I'm fine."

But something's not right. The apartment feels different. Lighter. Emptier. I notice Sam's stereo is gone. His shoes and boots by the front door are gone. Down the hall in the bedroom, I see a mess of clothes on the bed. None of them his.

I know before Mom says it. So I'm already smiling when she moans, "He's gone."

I'm smiling so hard, it hurts my face. I kneel down. "He's gone."

"No, you don't understand," she cries. "He left."

I hold her shoulders up, I look her in the eyes. I'm laughing. "He's gone!"

She falls into my arms and sobs. I hug her, and hug Ford, and I laugh. "He's really gone," I whisper. "I hope he never comes back."

generations

"This is a *good* thing, Luciana," Francesca says. Her car pulls in front of the comic-book store. Ford and Donald hop out and run inside. I walk slowly, 'cause I'm listening to the two sisters talk. "Sam is gone. This is a chance for you to start over."

Mom catches me as I hesitate outside the door. "Well, go on!"

Inside the comic-book store, the walls are adorned with posters of superheroes. Spider-Man, Thor, Captain America, Superman, and Wonder Woman in bold reds and blues. The reds and yellows of Flash, Iron Man, Robin, Human Torch, and Shazam. Brilliant yellow and bold black on the X-Men, my favorites. Usually the colors soothe me. But usually I come here alone.

Outside the window, Mom and Francesca speak. Francesca is holding her hand. Mom explains something, then raises her voice, then starts crying. Her sister hugs her.

Ford pulls on my arms. "Show me the Pokémon Pogs?"

"Sure," I say.

The store owner waves to me. His smile buried beneath a full beard. "X-Men, right?"

I nod. He points to a spinner rack near the front of the shop. "If you haven't read it, you'll love the Phalanx Covenant. Gold foil on the covers and everything."

My heart skips a beat when I pick up the issue with a preview of Generation X, art by Chris Bachalo. The lines, the curves, the action, the colors. All my years of reading, the familiar history of *X-Men* fills my mind with a kind of ease I find nowhere else.

My cousin pops up behind me, yanking it out of my hands. "Let me see!"

"Careful with it," I say. "Don't bend the pages."

"Why's the story called *Generation Next*?" he asks.

"Because it's the next generation of X-Men. They're kids like us, but mutants, with special powers."

"What's a generation?" Ford asks.

"It's a group of people born at the same time. Like Abuela is one generation. Her kids, like Mom and Francesca, are the next. Us three are the next, 'cause we're cousins. One day, when we all have kids, they'll be the next generation."

"*Generation Next*," Donald says, tossing the comic at me. He pushes Ford, saying, "Tag, you're it!" Ford chases him around the store.

"Cut it out," I moan, grabbing both of them by the back of their shirts. To the store owner, I say, "Sorry."

I pick up the comics, thumbing through the pages, wishing I had any of their powers. White Queen's telepathy, to erase

Mom's memories. Sabretooth's healing factor, to make my scars vanish. Husk's ability to metamorph into someone else. Blink, who can teleport to a new place, leaving the old behind. I'd even take stupid Jubilee's firework powers. Though I don't know how they'd help. Maybe they'd make Mom laugh.

Outside the window, Mom wipes at her tears. She waits outside while Francesca comes into the store. "Did ya'll find anything you wanted?"

Ford holds up a handful of pogs. Donald grabs a Superman comic off a shelf. I'm still holding the *Generation Next* books. I'm staring at them, reluctant to put them back. But I do. I make sure to put them back in the same racks where I got them.

"You don't want those?" Francesca asks.

"I do, but I don't have any money."

"Let me buy them."

"No, it's OK."

"Rex, I'm your aunt. Let me spoil you."

Mom comes inside. "He doesn't need those."

"Of course he doesn't need them," Francesca says, "but he wants them."

"Well, I want a lot of things and I don't get them," Mom argues.

"Well, you should change that."

Francesca sticks out her hand to me, and I give her the comic books. "Thank you."

Mom rolls her eyes and sneers at me.

After lunch, Francesca drives us to the video store, so we can rent a movie. She suggests her and Mom go get manicures next door. Mom laughs uncomfortably. "That kinda stuff is for rich people."

"No, it's not." Francesca smirks. "It's for women who want an hour to themselves. Life is short, Luciana. You have to treat yourself."

"You should do it," I say.

Mom flips around from the front seat, her teeth clamped down, a red look in her eyes. "Why? What's it to you?"

I don't say anything, 'cause I know everything's a wrong answer.

We turn into the strip mall lot. As Francesca parks, she turns up the radio. "Luciana, listen! This song! You need to hear this. It's perfect for you, for your situation. I want you to listen to every single word, every lyric."

It's "Hold On" by Wilson Phillips. It's a like a slow song for girls. But I know all the words. They play it on the radio a lot. Mom must know the words too, 'cause she starts singing them. So does Francesca. Then Donald joins. Then Mom is smiling. All the red goes out of her, and she's not Mom. She's Francesca's sister. She's that young girl again, the one I've seen in between moments, when Sam isn't around.

Her laughter is like church bells, her smile like sunshine.

I start singing too.

Mom reaches back and takes my hand. She squeezes it, singing the last line of the chorus, "*Hold on for one more day.*"

"*Shhhhh,*" I hiss.

"We're not being loud!" Mom snaps.

"If I can't hear the movie, then you are," I snap back.

I get up and turn the volume up on the TV. On my way back to the couch, I stick my tongue out. Mom sticks her tongue out back at me.

Hocus Pocus is playing on the VCR. I love this movie. I love anything with witches or superheroes or space. Or stuff that'll make me laugh. And this movie has witches and funny parts.

The whole apartment is dark. It's night outside, lights are off inside, except at the dining-room table, where Mom and Francesca are whispering underneath the one light that's on. Ford is in the velvet chair, one of his big toes in his mouth. I'm on one end of the couch. Donald is on the other, snoring.

Halfway through the movie, I note my aunt's giggles are gone. Replaced by slow, steady words. Like she's being cautious.

Mom whispers, "I don't remember that."

"You and I shared a room," Francesca says. "Your bed was on one side, mine was on the other. We were down the hall from our brother's room."

I don't want to be obvious. So I don't look up. But in the corner of my eye, Mom shakes her head no.

Francesca leans in. Her voice hushed. "He'd come in our room, late at night. Sit on the edge of my bed. I would pretend to be asleep. Then he'd go over to your bed—"

Mom says, "Our dad?"

Francesca nods.

"I don't—" Mom starts, shaking her head. She looks confused. Lost. Like she needs help remembering where she is. "He died in Vietnam."

"Before he died," Francesca says, "when we were girls."

Mom stares at the wall. Her eyes vacant. I don't mind

looking now, 'cause Mom is somewhere else. Maybe in Alaska, looking for her snow globe in the blizzard.

Francesca turns to me. I don't look away. Usually Francesca is smiling. Cheerful, happy. But now her eyes have a deeply sad look. She reaches over and takes Mom's hand. She squeezes it. "Luciana?"

A single tear runs down Mom's cheek. She whispers, "I don't remember."

Mom stands up. She uses the table to help. Walking over to me, without a glance in my direction, she asks, "Can I lie down?"

"Uh . . . sure." I stand up, thinking she means the couch. She doesn't move. Just stands there, looking off at nothing. Then she turns and walks down the hall into the pitch-black. And closes the bedroom door.

After the movie, I tuck Ford into his bunk. I let Donald have my old sleeping bag for the floor. I go to brush my teeth. I'm heading to bed when I see the dining room light is still on. Francesca is sitting beneath it. She looks at her hands.

I sit down where Mom was sitting.

"What doesn't Mom remember?"

"Our family," Francesca says to her hands.

The one light on in the apartment is directly above us. But it's one lightbulb. One. Against the pitch-black of the whole apartment. Of the night outside. The dark covering this whole side of the world. It feels like the shadows are pressing in on us, like the darkness is stirring just inches away. Hungry.

"His mom had to give him up when he was a boy," Francesca

says, still talking into her hands. "Did you know that about your grandfather? Because his mom wasn't mentally well. He went into the foster system as a young boy. He was in and out of homes. It was a different time then, the 1930s and '40s. I'm sure that terrible things happened to him. Changed him."

Francesca picks at her finger, at a nail bed. There's the remnants of red polish. Like an old car in a junkyard, with just the dirtiest hint of all the bright color it used to wear as it flashed by. Francesca tries to push the corner of her lips up, but falters. Like the weight of a smile is too much to sustain tonight.

Single mother. Schoolteacher. My aunt. Always so generous. But right now, she can't seem to muster words for me.

I reach out. Hold her hand.

She says, "Every generation has a choice to make. To pass on what they've learned. Or stop it. My third husband didn't have to drink. Or to hit me. He chose that. And I chose to stay with him for way too long. But then enough was enough. I had to make a choice. And I did. For my son. And now Luciana has to make that choice."

"But Sam left."

With one glance, Francesca makes me feel stupid. Naïve. Like I'm missing the big flashing sign that everyone can see but me.

"What?"

She shakes her head. "You'll see."

commute

"What happened to the car?" I ask.

It's early morning. The sun hasn't come up and there's still dew on the grass. I'm standing in front of our old Toyota hatchback. The front fender is gnarled and bent, crushed in places, streaked with black and red.

"Fender bender," Mom says.

Ford laughs. "Fender bender!"

I ask, "Are you OK?"

Mom shrugs it off. "Yeah. I'm fine."

As we get in the car, I buckle Ford into his car seat. I open my homework in my lap, but ask Mom, "Did the other person call the cops?"

"Why are you asking so many fucking questions?!" she shouts.

"'Cause I'm worried about the car insurance going up. It went up last time you rear-ended someone. And with Sam gone, we have less income, but the same amount of bills each month. So don't scream at me," I growl at her. "I'm trying to help."

She checks herself, then breathes. "I'm sorry. I'm stressed about money too. But Abuela is helping us. We're going to be fine."

It takes me a minute to pool my strength to ask, "Sam's not coming back . . . right?"

"No," she whispers. Then stronger: "No."

She adds, "We don't need him."

Hearing her say that should feel a certain way, like a wind chime in a gentle breeze. Calming. But something in Mom's tone, how she says it, sounds . . . wrong. Like a wind chime crashing onto the floor.

She turns on the radio and drives.

It's fifteen minutes to school. Twenty if there's construction on the highway. Ford is playing with his Power Rangers in the backseat. I'm double-checking my math homework. Mom is listening to the radio. It feels like any other morning.

Mom honks at another driver. Shouting, "Asshole!"

"What'd he do?" I ask.

"*Whose side are you on?!*" she shrieks.

"Mine."

Mom slaps me.

The angle isn't right, so it's more like getting hit with the butt of her palm. Unsatisfied, she slaps again. This time, from above, so it comes down on me. I flatten against the passenger door. She misses my face and hits my shoulder. She tries again, reaching for me, trying to keep her eyes on the road. When she goes to slap me again, she pulls the steering wheel and the whole car moves left. Horns blare and Ford squeals as the car swings toward oncoming traffic.

"Watch the fucking road!" I shout.

Mom jerks the wheel, and we go right, back into our own lane.

Behind us, a barrage of honking as Mom cuts off an eighteen-wheeler, flying onto the shoulder of the highway. Dirt and dust trail up around the car as she hits the brakes, and we snake-slide to a stop. Then her hand is coming down at me again and again. Slapping, slapping, slapping. My arms are up, my book falls from my lap, between my feet. Caught between her hand and my leg and the stick shift, my paper homework rips in half.

She undoes her seat belt. She's halfway across the tiny car, on top of me. There's a flurry of her fists and her palms until her elbow crashes into my nose. She's screaming these deep, guttural cries. Not anguish. Frustration. Like a football player, rushing forward in drills, slamming into the practice pads of blocking sleds. This isn't the real fight. This is a warm-up.

I'm not a son. Not her son.

I'm just something to hit.

The urge rises up in me. All it would take is one solid punch. Right in her nose. Maybe in her throat. Clock her so hard, she'd back off. Break her the way she's broken me.

I see my sister shaking her head: *No*.

And I drop my arms. I let Mom do it. Let her rail on me. Pound my chest, my arms, my face. Pummel me, get her aggression out.

It's what I deserve.

Until Ford cries, "Stop!"

Mom retreats back into her seat, gasping for air. Exhausted.

I feel the trickle of blood run out of my nose, down my lip, onto my yellow shirt. My eye blinks uncontrollably, already feeling bigger than usual. My skin burns from nails clawed down my arm.

Looking over at Mom, I ask, "Are you done?"

She slaps me again. "Fuck you!"

I open the car door and get out. I slam the door as hard as I can. I scream into the field of high grass to my right, roaring as loud and as long as I can until my throat goes raw and dry.

Several cows look up at me. They chew their cud. One of them moos.

"Get back in this car!" Mom shouts from behind me.

I start walking. Forward. Away from her. Toward school.

The car drives up beside me, half on the shoulder, half on the highway. Cars honk as they swing to avoid her. She calls out gently, "Rex, get in the car. You can't walk on the side of the highway. It's dangerous."

She's dangerous. I go to respond, but feel my lip already swelling. The familiar metallic taste in my mouth. I shake my head.

Now she's shouting. "Fine! Then walk to school!" My backpack is thrown out the window. The car takes off, kicking dirt in my face as she peels out onto the highway. More honking, and shouting. My heart tugs, thinking of Ford.

I feel sick all the way to school.

The hallways are empty. It's still early, even though I'm late to my zero-hour class. When I walk in, Mrs. Telford jumps, grabbing her chest. "Rex, are you OK?"

"Sorry, I'm late."

I take my seat.

Mrs. Telford stares. My classmates stare. I get out my book, my notepad, my pencil. I write down the dates on the board. I don't feel anything. Except the pressure from the hand-built wall inside me, holding back an ocean of pain. The wall is solid enough. Even as blood drips from my nose onto my history notes.

When the bell rings, Mrs. Telford dismisses the class, but stops me. "Rex, please, tell me what happened."

"It's nothing," I say.

"Yes, it is. Please, you have to tell me so I can help."

I don't say anything.

Her face is stretched with lines. Each one reminds me of the history timelines she shows us, moving into the past and the future as the lines run off the pages' end. She has white hair. Red lipstick. Small pearl earrings. She's old, probably Abuela's age. So I've never noticed how pretty she is, with the kindness in her eyes. I bet she's a good mother.

She asks, "Are you being bullied by another student?"

I laugh. "I wish."

When I get home, Mom is waiting for me at the dining-room table. She rushes over and throws her arms around me. I don't move to defend myself, or to accept the hug. I just stand there. It feels like I'm standing beside my body.

Like I'm standing in the same space as my sister. Not alive. Not dead. A ghost. Except my sister is dead. I wonder if I'm dead too.

'Cause even though Mom's hugging me, I can't feel it.

She's saying, "About this morning—I was in a bad mood. I'm just stressed."

My body is looking at her, but my swollen lip doesn't say anything. The purple around my right eye is faint. Tomorrow it will be the same color as Ronald McDonald's friend Grimace. I like the Hamburglar way more. The Fry Guys too.

Mom is pleading with me, taking my hands, but I don't hear whatever she's saying. I don't care.

She hands me a new CD. "I bought this for you. As an apology."

I stare at it in my hands. The band is called Enigma. The word means puzzles. I remember one of the songs from a movie called *Sliver* with Sharon Stone.

Mom asks, "Well?"

My body stares at her.

She asks, "Do you forgive me?"

I shake my head. "No. I'm done forgiving. Because you'll just do it again."

barbecue

"Just take off tonight," I say. "It's going to be fun. All the neighbors are getting together for a barbecue to celebrate the long weekend for Memorial Day."

Mom huffs. "I wish I could. But it's Friday, best night of the week for tips. I can't skip. But you and Ford go. Have fun. But no swimming."

"It's a pool party!" Ford says.

"I don't care. I don't want y'all in the pool when I'm at work. What if something happens?"

"Nothing will happen," I say.

Ford repeats, "Nothing will happen."

Mom grabs her ironed waitress apron and her car keys. She points a finger at us, the one that's never healed right, so it actually points off to the side. "*NO. SWIMMING.*"

I say, "Understood."

Ford throws himself on the ground and kicks his feet in the air. "You suck!"

"Bye," Mom says, walking out the door and closing it behind her.

In the canyon between apartment buildings, the sun's already set. But the sky and clouds overhead are shifting from blue and white to orange and red and yellow, the color of melting sherbet.

All of the neighbors come out for the party. Charlotte and Scott and their two daughters, Amber and Cecily. Elena and Esmerelda and their parents. Ricky, his mom and dad. The Austins. Brad and Alice, who live upstairs. The Muñoz sisters and their three kids who live across the breezeway. Missy and her mom. Florence and her husband, Dale. Jasmine and some others.

The parents and other adults make a big mob around the courtyard table with the booze, the radio, and the snacks. Us kids dart in and out under their elbows to grab paper bowls full of pretzels, chips, and popcorn. Then run back to the side of the pool where we've built a circle with the plastic recliners.

I like to take one chair and flip it upside down onto another, so the two chairs make a 69. If you add two more, then throw towels over it, you can pretend you're in a spaceship, which Ford likes. So I build a spaceship, and let him and the other littles play.

Us big kids sit nearby—too cool to play games with the littles and not mature enough to hang with the adults.

We're playing Truth or Dare, when Missy says, "I dare you to jump in the pool."

"No way. My mom would find out and crucify me. Think of another."

"Ugh. Fine." Missy considers and then her eyes light up. "OK, I dare you and Teddy to get an ice cube and hold it in the groove of your arm, you know, the opposite of your elbow, between your bicep and your forearm—yeah, right there—and hold it as long as you can."

"How did I get roped into this?" Teddy asks.

"Just do it, you big baby," Sadie says.

I ask, "Why? What's it do?"

With a devilish grin, Missy says, "You'll see."

I do it. After a few minutes, it starts to hurt. Teddy and I are making faces at each other, to see who will crack first. Teddy is much bigger than me, even though he's six months younger. We wrestle in the pool all the time, and it's always a competition. This is no different. He's bigger, but I can take more pain.

After one minute and fifty-seven seconds, Teddy opens his arm, squealing. "That burns!"

I keep holding mine. Let the cold feel like fire, biting at my skin. I stare at Missy, smiling. She's looking between me and her wristwatch timer. "Three minutes . . . think you can do four?"

"I can do it 'til it melts," I say as ice water drips down my elbow.

We're all laughing, me 'cause it really is hurting but in a way that I control. That's when we hear the parents whispering. Everyone looking at me before raising their gaze to see someone I can't 'cause I'm sitting down.

But I hear Charlotte say, "Rex, it's Sam."

I stand up, the ice falling from the crook in my arm, which has turned bright red, glistening wet. My arm from the elbow down feels like there is ice in my veins. I shiver when I see Sam, leaving Kendra's apartment.

When he sees me, he says, "H-h-hey, Rex. C-c-can I see Ford?"

I realize Ford and the other littles are still inside their spaceship, oblivious to the rest of the world. Beneath the towels, we hear squeals and laser blasts made from lips and tongues pressed together.

"No, Sam. You can't."

I walk out of the pool area, letting the metal gate slam shut behind me. Sam's eyes blink hard at the sound. With him not living under my roof, with the neighbors watching, I feel a rush of strength, of bravery. I wonder if this is how superheroes feel when they first set their sights on the bad guy.

"Wh-where i-is he, Rex? I know m-my s-son's here. L-luciana's at w-work, so you're w-watching him."

I shrug. "Exactly. Mom's at work. Which means I'm in charge. And I don't have to tell you anything."

Sam's fists squeeze tight. "W-watch y-your t-tone."

"Or what?" My feet surprise me when they take two steps forward, bringing me within his reach. "You'll beat me in front of everyone? Be my guest."

The song from Disney's *Beauty and the Beast*, "Be Our Guest," plays in my head. I actually laugh out loud.

This makes Sam even more angry. The vein in his forehead bulges, his skin brightens to the color of the apple given to Snow White by the evil queen. Only now, I'm the one doing the tempting, repeating Sam's favorite line back to him. "Come on, big man. Think you can take me?"

Missy is at the bars of the poolyard. She whispers, "Rex."

This is more fuel to feed the flame. I can feel the wicked smirk growing on my face. The audience makes me fearless. I feel a storm brewing. I welcome it.

Kendra comes up behind Sam, rubbing his arm. She whispers, "Don't, Sam."

And I'm shouting, "Why not? He does it all the time."

With a deep breath, Sam contains himself. "I j-j-just w-want t-to s-see my s-son."

"And?" I'm shouting, not able to control the volume. "You should have thought of Ford *before* you started smacking me and Mom around, before you left like a coward. Funny that, all those times you called my dad a pussy and a coward for leaving, and you did the same damn thing. Guess you're not so different."

Sam steps forward, his chest bumping mine. He's glaring. "St-stop i-it, Rex."

"No, Sam." I push forward, not backing down. He could crush me. But I won't go down without a fight. And he'll have to do it in front of everyone. "Fuck you, man. Get the fuck out of here. Before I call the cops."

The storm brewing inside me is here. Bigger, darker than I thought.

I put up a wall to contain it, to control it, but it wants out. It won't be controlled. It's too late anyway 'cause I put all my strength into my body and push forward, shoving him as hard as I can. Then I'm screaming in public, just like Mom.

"Go on! Get out of here! You're not in charge here. Not anymore. You're out of our lives. You're done. We're done with you. Go! Get the fuck out of here! No one wants you here!"

"N-not t-til I s-see my son."

"No! He doesn't need you. He doesn't need to see what you do."

"Wh-what d-do I d-do?"

I hear the loudest laughter ringing in my ear, and discover it's mine, cackling madly. "What do you do? You destroy things, Sam. You beat them to a bloody pulp. Do you know how many times I've cleaned up Mom's bleeding noses and lips. How many ice packs I've made for her bruises? How many broken fingers I've had to splint? And that just her. Do you want to talk about what you've done to *me*?"

"I-It's th-the alcohol. I-I'm s-sick."

Laughter again. Mine again. "You're sick? Me too! Sick of your shit. So get THE FUCK out of here. FUCKING NOW."

Kendra steps forward. "You need to show some respect. Sam is dealing with his own demons and he wants to make them right."

"Kendra, what the fuck are you even doing protecting him? You two aren't friends."

"I'm his sponsor."

"His what?!"

"Alcoholics Anonymous," she says. "He's trying to get better. He wants to make amends."

Still more laughter, coming up from my throat like vomit. "Amends? He wants to fix things? SO FIX ME, SAM! GO ON! YOU THINK YOU CAN PUT ME BACK TOGETHER?!"

I'm screaming so hard, the rest of the world is a blur. To the right, I sense the littles have stopped playing. From their spaceship, they're peeking out, seeing monsters in real life. Ford with them. I hate that he's seeing me like this. But it's too late. It's all coming out.

Some of the parents are moving to shield their children. Scott and Charlotte are approaching me from behind. I feel

Charlotte's hand on my shoulder. A kind whisper, "Rex, let him leave."

"NO!" I scream, not taking my eyes from Sam. "I WANNA HEAR THIS APOLOGY THAT'S GOING TO MAKE EVERYTHING ALL BETTER! LET'S HEAR IT, SAM!!"

He can't even look me in the face when he stutters, "I-I-I'm s-s-sorry."

"FOR WHAT?!"

"H-h-hitting y-you. H-h-hurting y-you."

"AND WHAT ABOUT MY SISTER? ARE YOU SORRY FOR HER? IS YOUR APOLOGY GOING TO BRING HER BACK FROM THE DEAD?"

Someone turns off the radio. There's no sound in the apartment complex. People are watching. Listening. Horrified. But their horror is nothing compared to mine.

Kendra tries to pull Sam away. She would have better luck with a mountain. "Sam—"

Now Sam is unleashed, showing his true nature, screaming so hard, his stutter vanishes. "FUCK YOU, YOU LITTLE SHIT. YOU DON'T KNOW WHAT HAPPENED THAT NIGHT!"

Charlotte and Scott are holding me back, as I shriek, "YOU KILLED HER! MOM WAS PREGNANT AND YOU PUNCHED HER. AND MARISA DIED. SHE'S DEAD, 'CAUSE OF YOU!"

Kendra and Brad and Dale are holding Sam back. Even with three adults, and now Elena's dad, he's still moving forward, inch by inch, screaming, "YOU THINK YOU KNOW, BUT YOU DON'T. YOU DON'T KNOW THE WHOLE

STORY!! AND YOU'VE NEVER EVEN BOTHERED TO ASK, HAVE YOU? ASK ME, I'LL TELL YOU THE REAL TRUTH! I DARE YOU!"

There's twenty feet between us, our neighbors dragging us away from each other, even as we pull toward each other, like magnets powered by pain—by the same pain.

I'm still screaming, but my strength is draining. I've used too much, too fast, but I'm still shouting, "You killed her! You killed my sister. And it broke me. It broke Mom."

Sam is crying, still fighting to come at me. I don't know if he wants to kill me or hug me. But he's shouting. "I-i-it b-broke m-me too. I-i-it b-broke a-all of u-us."

Kendra is saying, "Sam, let's get out of here, I'll drive."

Charlotte is whispering to me, "Rex, it's OK. You're OK now. He's leaving. You're safe."

Safe? I've never been safe. And I'm not sure I ever will be.

My whole body is sweat and strained muscles and screaming, as I gasp for air, not breathing, trying to get out the words I've been holding onto for so long, "I am broken 'cause of you! I want to die. I want you to die. You piece of shit. You fucking has-been. You fucking asshole. What have you done with your life, huh? Besides beat me and my mom for the last decade? Huh? Fucking nothing."

And Sam, being pulled behind the corner, takes one last look at me, meeting my eyes, and says, "I've b-been r-raising you."

"By using me as a punching bag?!" I call.

He cries back. "I-I d-did the b-best I c-could."

Then he's gone.

And I realize my face is soaked in tears.

stalker

The last bell of the school day rings.

From my locker, I grab the books I need for homework. Which is all of them. I heave the backpack up, starting down the hall toward the cafeteria to wait for my bus.

Funny how the lunchtime tension vanishes after school. Everyone's too excited to head home. Friends sit together, write notes, share homework answers, ask each other on dates. Students are all smiling, happy to leave school, to return to loving families and safe homes.

I'd rather stay here.

Alison, Cara, and Ethan wave at me from our usual spot by the third pillar. This is where we sit and wait together, until they call the numbers for our buses.

Alison and I discuss re-creating the Greek pantheon for modern times. We agree there should be a Goddess Spudra, queen of potatoes. "I mean, everyone loves potatoes, right? Mashed, baked, buttered, French fried—"

"Tater tots!"

"Goddess Spudra! We supplicate thee for——"

"Supplicate?"

"It's on my vocab test this week."

"Why do we have to learn words we'll never use again?"

"'Cause it makes us sound smarter?"

I soak up the last bits of laughter, like a hungry man soaking up the last of soup with bread. Stockpiling smiles in my chest like a squirrel before winter. Like a battery, charging now so I'll have some light later—in the darkness.

Cara eats Skittles from the vending machine. Even though she's Mormon, Alison sneaks a sip of Cara's soda. Ethan catches her with a glance. "Hey! I thought you can't have caffeine!"

"It was hardly a sip!"

Ethan cackles, "The devil has swayed you!"

"Wait, does that make me the devil for buying soda?" Cara asks.

I say, "We should definitely have a Greek god of wicked diets. Soda, coffee, sugary candy, potato chips—or would those fall under Queen Spudra's domain?"

We're all laughing, until Alison freezes. Her eyes narrow on me. No, not at me. Past me. "Uh . . . Rex, is that your mom?"

The hair on the back of my neck stands up.

I don't want to, but I turn.

Mom is here. At school. Not at the office, where some parents come. She's here, in the cafeteria, where I've never seen any parent. She's out of place. A shark swimming among a school of fish. Only it's my school.

I feel sick.

What is she doing here? Is she going to attack me? Scream at me? Hit me? Make a scene? Tell me how much she hates me? That I'm not welcome to come home?

My whole body feels heavy, like I've been thrown into ice water.

But Mom crouches behind a pillar. Hiding. She scans the crowd, then scurries to the next pillar, keeping low. She's hunched, like movie soldiers trying to remain unseen in a battlefield. The whole time, Mom is staring past me—out the glass doors at the buses.

Then I know why.

I get up, running to her. "You can't be here. You have to leave."

"Shhhh." Her eyes dart around, frantic. She gazes past me, eyes locked on the buses. "I'm going to give Sam a piece of my mind."

Students walk by—slowing, staring.

My hands open in front of me, gently, but with command in them. "No. No, Mom, you can't do that here. This is my school. I go here."

"I know. He'll never expect it. What's his bus number?"

"I'm not telling you. You have to leave. Please. Do *not* make a scene here."

More students are staring. Confused by the intruder.

A teacher takes notice. Secretly I pray the teacher will call the cops and my mom will be escorted out the way she came. That would be better than her confronting Sam.

A snicker. Two girls are laughing at my mom, at her appearance. Flip-flops, cut-off sweatshorts, an oversized Simpsons shirt. No makeup, no perfume, unshowered. Mom's self-dyed hair tied into a ball on top of her head by a rubber band. The crazed look in her eyes.

Over the loudspeaker, a voice announces, "Bus 268 arriving. Bus 268."

Mom smiles.

She charges forward. I could have grabbed her, but that might have made it worse. She might have attacked. Maybe if she runs out, if her and Sam fight, they'll both go to jail. And no one will know about me. My connection to the scene that's about to take place.

There's a blur of yellow-orange and black stripes. Bus 268 pulls up, Sam behind the oversized wheel. Mom is hiding behind the pillar closest to the doors.

Students line up. Mom bends down, getting in line. Students laugh, looking at her with confusion. She puts a cracked-skin finger over her lips, saying, "*Shhhh*." She smiles. This is a game to her.

Another teacher notices, saying, "Excuse me, ma'am——"

The door to Bus 268 opens. The first few students get on board. Six, maybe eight students take their seats.

I stand there, like a lighthouse overlooking the sea, knowing a violent storm is about to hit land. But there's nothing I can do. A lighthouse can't stop a storm.

The teacher steps closer, saying, "Ma'am, who are you? You can't get on that bus!"

Mom shoulder-smashes past her, pushing two, then three, students out of her way. She runs onto the bus.

Then Luciana starts screaming. "How dare you come back to our apartment! You stay away from me! You stay away from

Ford! You stay away from Rex!" For added effect, she points at me.

With my name, already, there's not much mistaking who she's talking about. But the pointed accusation confirms her case. As she continues screaming, the students on the bus all look out their windows to stare at me.

alone

It's almost noon. Mom is awake, but she hasn't gotten out of bed. I cross the living room, turn the volume up on the TV so Ford doesn't hear her crying. But the louder the TV gets, the louder she does too. Her cries turn into moans, which turn into sobs, which turn into shrieks until I go back there.

"What? Why are you being like this?"

"I'm so alone," she whispers, pulling the sheets and blankets over herself.

"No, you're not. Ford and I are here. And you need to go to work. We need money for groceries."

"Where's Sam?"

"He's gone. You know that."

She wails.

I snap, "Cut it out! You're freaking Ford out!"

"So?!" she yells. "You don't know the pain I'm feeling."

"Because Sam is gone? If he were here, you'd be in more pain, 'cause he'd kick the shit out of you for acting like this."

She flies at me faster than I can blink, and seizes my chin in her grip. "Watch your mouth. You will not talk to me like that!"

I wrestle her fingers off my face. When I try to step away, she leaps on my back, a giant mosquito, desperate for attention.

"Get off me!" I shout, peeling her hands off from around my neck. She finds her feet, standing there in panties and a bra, both brown, one lighter, one darker than her pale stomach skin. I don't want to see this. I don't want to see her like this. I turn away. "Shower. Get dressed. Go to work. Be normal."

She shoves me hard into her door. When I stumble back, there's a smear of blood on the door from my nose that looks like an inkblot test, like a butterfly, its wings spraying out to take flight. When Mom flips me around, she slaps me, saying, "Hit me back!"

"What? No!"

"You think you can tell me what to do! Make me!"

"Stop it!" I scream. "I'm not Sam. I won't hit you!"

She slaps me again.

Blood drains into my mouth from my nose. Maybe a broken lip.

I hate this. I hate the taste of metal. The familiarity of it. And I hate her. I hate her for being like this. So I spit.

My blood sprays all over her face. Now she looks like how I feel.

Then she's on me, her hand coming down again and again. Not a fist, but an open palm.

Slap.

Slap.

Slap.

Slap.

Slap.

Slap.

Slap.

Slap.

Slap.

Until she collapses on the carpet next to me, crying. She curls inward, cradling her knees in a fetal position. The sight of it, the sight of the shape of anyone like that, my mind goes to one place. My sister. In Mom's tummy. All those years ago.

Vulnerable. Tiny, but growing. Oxygen through blood. An umbilical cord tying her to Mom, connecting them in some way I'll never know. Sharing blood. Life. Until—

I shudder.

I think about what Sam said, at the barbecue, about what the whole story is. And I feel more sick, because for so long, I've wanted to know, but couldn't ask. But lately? Lately, it's flipped. More than I don't want to ask, I desperately *need* to know.

I stand up, watching Mom, wailing on the floor, sobbing, the same way she did the first time I found her, curled up on the living-room floor in another apartment in another town, before Ford, before Marisa, but after Sam.

Like then, she whimpers now. Whispering through snot and saliva and tears, "Tell me you love me. Tell me everything will be OK."

My six-year-old self said it. He said, "It'll be OK. I love you." He said it over and over and over, time after time after time.

But I am not six anymore.

I've lost too much to be that young.

"Tell me everything will be OK," she says again, "Tell me you love me."

I want to. I want to say it. But I'm done lying. Standing over her, I say, "No."

She lets out a wail, like I kicked her. She tears at her hair, pulling out a clump of the fine brown strands with blond highlights, shrieking, "I'm so alone . . . so alone."

I don't say it, but I think it: *So am I.*

Then Marisa is there. She pets Mom's head.

And without lying, I say, "You're not alone. Not if you don't choose to be."

the return

My shoulders ache from the long walk home from the store. With the six plastic grocery bags in my hand, I struggle to open the door. The knob turns just enough, and gives.

As I tip inside, my heart freezes and my fingers release. The bags drops, the milk gallon bounces once then twice, thankfully not spilling. Though it crushes the loaf of bread. I don't care. 'Cause all I can see is Sam sitting on our couch.

Mom looks at me, her hand in his, and says, "Rex, we need to—"

I'm shouting, "NO. No fucking way!"

Sam is saying, "Th-there's g-going t-to b-be s-some changes 'r-round here—"

Mom is saying, "We've been talking and it's the best for Ford, and you—"

But I have my hands to my ears, blocking out their words, shouting, "No! I can't do this. I won't do this anymore. Why are you two doing this to each other?!"

Sam stands up, about to extend his hand. Thinks better of it, takes his hand back, sits back down.

And I'm still saying, "No, no, no, no, no, no."

Mom says, "Rex, stop it. You're being immature."

I call out, "Why?! Do you two want to be miserable? I don't."

"We're going to work at it," Mom says.

"N-n-no more f-fighting," Sam says.

"And no more screaming matches," Mom adds.

And I'm saying, "Never gonna happen."

Mom stands up, putting her hands on my arms, making me listen, some weird calm in her voice, like she's possessed by a politician or a preacher. And she says, "This is happening. So get on board."

silence

A month goes by. I don't say a word. Not a single word. I've read about silent protests somewhere, and it works for me. I enjoy it. Pissing off Mom. Not answering Sam's questions. I keep waiting for them to hit me. Mom gets close a few times, but doesn't.

Sam doesn't either. Forty-six days sober.

But nothing lasts forever.

fireworks

Fourth of July, Ford and I light fireworks in the pool area with our neighbors. The sparks whiz and spin and fly into the air and explode. When I look back, Mom and Sam are holding hands. They look younger in the light of the pool at night.

They smile.

Which pisses me off.

what happened

I cook the ground beef until all the pink has been replaced by brown. I sprinkle specks of black pepper, which stays. The white salt vanishes on contact. I add the Hamburger Helper powder and pasta along with a cup of water and stir.

With mom at work, I only pull out three paper plates. I serve the food at the table. Ford and Sam watch the TV. I read a book. When we're done, I clean up.

A knock at the door. Elena and Esmerelda ask if Ford can come over. Sam says yes.

When the kitchen is clean, I start to walk back to my room. Sam says, "Rex. C-can w-we t-talk?"

I point to my mouth, and shrug.

He pats the chair in the dining room, next to his. "Th-then I'll talk."

I don't want to.

"P-p-please," he says. "I'm o-on S-step Eight. I gotta m-make amends. That m-means telling you e-everything."

I sit.

And he says he'll tell me everything.

Sam holds a hand up, like he's in court, swearing he'll tell me the truth. I think, his truth, at least.

First, he asks, did I know Luciana had been stalking him?

The last week of school, she showed up at his work, at the bus barn—the place where the buses sleep at night. She stormed inside and demanded to see Sam. He was still on his route; he wasn't there. When his boss told Luciana, she lost it. She got in her car, locked the doors, and sat there, waiting for him to return.

When his bus pulled into the large fenced-in lot, Luciana began honking her horn. Once she had his attention, she drove the car into his motorcycle. She knocked it over. She reversed the car, then drove into it again. And again. And again, until it was smashed into the wall and her front fender was gnarled.

By this time, someone had closed the gates.

Luciana tried to flee, but there was nowhere to go. She drove around the bus lot in circles until the police came. They would have arrested her, but Sam refused to press charges.

A week later, she showed up at his new apartment. She kicked in the door and smashed all of the new dishes Doris had bought for him. Then Mom ripped up all of his clothes. Sam says he did not touch her. He let her. He deserved it.

A week after that, she followed him to an Alcoholics Anonymous meeting. She interrupted the meeting, screaming that she knew he was having an affair with Kendra. She wasn't his sponsor, she was a slut. Kendra stole her man. Mom was escorted out of the meeting, out of the church basement, and asked not to return or the cops would be called.

Sam said he was embarrassed, but he was glad it happened.

'Cause it made him open up for the first time. It made him tell
his story.

What happened to his daughter,

my sister,

Marisa.

"I n-never wanted kids," Sam says. "N-not 'til I met you,
Rex. You were so smart, so bright. F-funny too.

"Then Luciana told me she w-was pregnant. I'd n-never
been so happy. I was excited. I wanted a boy, a son. But when
we found out it was a girl? I was surprised at how h-happy I was.
I'm one of four boys. All we did was fight. I thought, a daughter
would be cool.

"But a kid m-means m-money. So I got a s-second job. And
a th-third. Maintenance man, p-pizza delivery, lifeguarding. I
w-wanted to save up as much cash as I could. Luciana needed to
cut back h-her hours as a police dispatcher. So I worked.

"That's wh-when your abuela sent you away for the summer.
S-sent you to your d-dad's parents in Tennessee.

"You w-were gone. Luciana was w-working. I was w-working,
like a dog. And one night, I just n-needed a drink.

"I knew I shouldn't. 'Cause one drink leads to two, lead to
four, leads to—I d-didn't want to be my dad. Not with Luciana
eight months pregnant.

"But I did it anyways. I went to a b-bar.

"When I came home, Luciana took one whiff of my breath
and started screaming. You know how she is. She knows how to
get a man worked up . . . she drives him to do . . ." Sam says. He
looks me in the eyes.

In my head, I say, *I've never hit her back.*

Sam nods. He knows what my eyes say. "I know you haven't.

You're b-better than me." He hesitates. "Y-you know your d-dad h-hit her too? Call him and ask. B-better yet, call your grand-mother. She knows."

I shrug. Then I recall what Francesca said in Abilene.

Sam nods again. He takes a deep breath. Something in his face, in his body, says he's telling all the truths he knows. Step 8. He's not doing it for me or for Mom. He's doing it for himself. For God. If he lies, he's fucked. So he has to tell the truth.

"You kn-know your mom, she knows h-how to get in there, with her words I mean. How to c-cut through to the soul. She's g-got this knack for figuring out what makes people t-tick, what a person's weakness is, just how to hit the nail right on the head j-just right . . .

"So I'm drunk, and she's shouting at me . . ." Big, large tears well up at Sam's eyes. "She's slapping me, and c-c-calling m-me a pussy. Same a-as my d-dad u-used to c-call me. And I l-lost it." And he's crying now. His face reddened, confessing. "I ain't g-gonna m-make no excuses. I d-did it, Rex. I p-punched her. I h-hit her."

Sobbing, he says, "I d-d-didn't want to. B-but she got inside my head. That's how we did, f-fight and make up, f-fight and make up. It was this . . . this vicious cycle. And . . . and . . . and I was drunk. D-devil in the bottle was inside me. My d-daddy was inside me. All that p-poison in me m-made me do it. But it was my h-hand. My fist. I d-did it. 'S my f-fault."

He's sobbing.

Wipes his tears. Adds, "But. . . ."

Sam fixes on my gaze and says, "It's L-luciana's f-fault too."

Suddenly I'm all anger. Sam is the one who hit her. It's his fault. He did the hitting.

. . . but Mom hits him too. She hits me.

Are they monsters for the violence? Or are the monsters the people who made Mom and Sam the way they are?

Sam continues, "'Cause she p-pushed me. 'Cause she always p-pushes me. She screams, and she slaps, and she won't let go. Like a hook that's got a f-fish, and no m-matter how hard that f-fish struggles, that hook is in its l-lip, and it's n-not gonna let go. That f-fish is already done-for."

Sam says, "I n-never hit a woman b-before your mom. Never. Then I met her, and I was d-done-for. I knew she was t-trouble. M-maybe that's what m-made me love her. 'Cause on some l-level? She was j-just like my dad. Said all the s-same cruel things he used to. And I h-hurt her the s-same way my father h-hurt me."

He says, "M-maybe we were m-meant for each other. M-maybe we b-belong together. 'Cause I'm f-fucked up. And so is she."

He adds, "P-pain is a bond. And w-we've hurt each other too much, to j-just leave it now. T-to g-give up. So I came back."

He says, "F-for her.

"F-for Ford.

"F-for you.

"Y-y'all're m-my family."

Is this it? A cycle of pain? He hurts Mom, she hurts me, I hurt . . . everyone around me?

I feel sick to my stomach. My whole body tingling, hurting, I feel like I might float away. 'Cause for once, my sister isn't here in the room. And I want her to confirm it. I want anyone to tell me if the story is true.

Or if this is just the closest I'll get to the truth.

'Cause Mom doesn't remember anything.

And no one else was there.

I was gone. Which is why I say: "It was my fault too."

My voice cracks, 'cause I haven't spoken in so long. I continue, "'Cause I wasn't there."

Sam looks at me like I'm speaking in tongues. He says, without a stutter, "Rex. It's not your fault."

I say, "It is."

He shakes his head no. "The blame b-belongs to m-me and L-luciana. N-no one else. Y-you were just a kid."

He says, "We did it. Y-your mom st-started the fight. I f-finished it. But it w-was us. It was an accident. But we killed her. Not you."

Every inch of me goes numb—and on fire. Like I might shatter, or explode. Dizzy. I get up. I stumble to my room. Close my door.

"You h-hear me?" Sam calls after me. "It's not your fault."

And I cry.

And I can't stop crying.

I lie there, like my mom, in the fetal position, sobbing. The ocean overcomes the walls inside me. Floodgates open. And I cry.

scissors

Ethan and his dad drop me off outside the turquoise-painted apartment fence. As their sedan reverses, I wave. On the gate keypad, I punch in the code. The gate opens. I weave in and out from under the trees through the parking lot, trying to avoid the hot August sun as I make my way toward my building.

Mom is talking to Charlotte as they hover between cars. They're whispering and laughing. Sometimes I forget how pretty Mom's smile is. When she sees me, she turns to Charlotte and puts her finger up to her mouth and goes, "*Shhh*. Keep it a secret, OK? See you at four."

Mom jogs over. She's wearing her usual: an old shirt, cut-off sweats, and flip-flops. Her hair is up in a little bunch on the top of her head, like Pebbles from *The Flintstones*. Mom gives me a side hug. "How was your slumber party?"

"Slumber parties are what girls do. I just slept over."

"Isn't that the same thing?" Mom asks, poking me.

"What were you and Charlotte whispering about?"

"Just a little thing we're having this afternoon."

"What thing?"

"Just a little summer barbecue," Mom says. But her lips pinch together in a trapped smile, the way she does when she wants to say something but doesn't. When we walk in the apartment, she says, "But stay out of the fridge."

"Why?"

"Just don't go in there." She gives me a full-on hug, then a push toward my room.

Ford and Sam are playing Duck Hunt on Nintendo. I lean down and hug Ford, whispering into his ear, "What's in the fridge?"

Swiping me away, he moans, "Go away! I'm winning!"

Mom gets on the phone in the kitchen, dials, then starts whispering to another neighbor. I'm hanging out, trying to listen for clues when Mom catches me. She swats at me playfully, mouthing the words, *Stop hovering! Go!*

Saturday mornings, I usually go see if any of the other kids in the complex want to hang out. But today I decide to hang out at home. I pull my comics out of the closet, lay in bed on my side, and read. Between pages, I listen outside my room. When Mom says she has to run back to the store for something, I wait until she leaves. Then I walk out, grab a glass from the cabinet, and open the fridge to get water.

"H-how'd you d-do that?!" Sam asks Ford, focused on the game.

Ford's just laughing.

The bottom shelf of the fridge has a large Kroger box inside.

There's a tiny plastic window on top through which I see "*Happy Birth*—" in purple pastel icing letters on white frosting. The muscles in my jaw tense, and I realize I'm smiling.

I close the fridge, then go back to my room. I'm excited for later, for the barbecue.

The neighbors are all gathered around Dale's back patio and his grill. The men are drinking beers, the women drinking wine coolers. Except Florence, who is practically a hundred years old and drinks beer. Mom doesn't drink alcohol, but has Coke from a red Solo cup. The radio is turned up. None of the neighbors complain, because everyone is invited.

Ford and the other little kids are playing Pin the Tail on the Donkey. They don't use an actual pin anymore 'cause last time Elena stabbed her mom in the leg when she was blindfolded. She screamed bloody murder and Elena got spanked in front of everyone. Now the tail has a piece of tape on it instead.

The older kids my age, we're all in the pool, having chicken fights. Sadie is on my shoulders, and Missy is on Teddy's shoulders. Even though it's against the rules, Missy keeps splashing water in my eyes and pulling my hair. I use my foot like a hook around Teddy's leg and Sadie pushes Missy. When the other teams fall backward, Missy kicks me in the face.

I grab my face. "Oh shit!"

"Language!" Mom shouts from the other side of the pool fence.

"Rex, your nose!" Missy cries. She swims over and tilts my head back, staring at my face. "You're bleeding everywhere."

Ribbons of bright crimson are rushing down my wet body

into the water. As the blood trails away in swirls, it stains the water. I realize my life is just a series of annoying nosebleeds.

"Get out of the pool before you give us AIDS," Teddy says.

Sadie pushes him. "Don't be a jerk. Only gays get AIDS."

"Exactly," Teddy says, splashing me.

I splash him back.

"Come on, out of the pool," Missy says.

"Here," says Florence, rushing over with a roll of paper towels. "Make sure to tilt his head back. You OK, Rex?"

"I'm fine," I say. "It's nothing."

Missy rolls up two paper towels into a sword shape, and shoves it up my nose. "Ow!" I moan. "Be gentle!"

"What happened?!" Mom screeches when she sees the red all down my chin and my chest and stomach.

"I'm fine. Just a bloody nose," I say. "Looks worse than it is 'cause I'm all wet."

Mom lets out a frustrated squeal, then turns to Charlotte, laughing. "Just wait until yours are teenagers. They'll make you go crazy too."

Missy sits with me while Teddy and Sadie corral the other kids in the pool area to play Marco Polo. "I'm really sorry," she says.

"It's totally fine," I say. "It was an accident, right?"

"Maybe," she says sarcastically. "Though you often deserve a good kick in the face."

"Not with your big feet. You could kill a man with those."

"Hey! I have dainty lady feet!"

"Do you?" I ask.

"Says the boy with hair longer than mine."

I push my long hair out of my face and back around my ear. "This is the look!"

"If you're in a metal band, maybe." We're both laughing.

The smell of cooking meat drifts through the air and hits my one working nostril. The scent of burger patties and hot dogs makes my mouth water. Past Missy, I see Scott and Charlotte setting up a long table. There's a veggie platter, bowls of chips—potato and corn—and dips, some salsa, a seven-layer bean dip, pretzels, cookies, a bunch of two-liter bottles of soda, and ketchup and mustard alongside a giant jar of pickles.

"Let's snack," Missy says. She grabs my hand and pulls me along after her.

We stand in the sun, letting our bathing suits dry while we devour the salty chips and the sugary soda. When the meats are ready, the crowd descends on the table like flies. Missy and I cut ahead to get first pick. She likes her burgers so raw they're bleeding. I like mine so well-done, they're burned and crispy.

With full mouths, we lower our heads and blush, embarrassed by our moms dancing together to an old song on the radio. "Adults are so weird."

"So weird," I say.

"When you're my age, you'll realize adults are just kids in bigger bodies," Florence says from behind us. She sits down next to us and pulls a cigarette from a small red leather wallet like my grandma June used to. She tucks it in her lips and lights it. "No matter how old you get, you're still acting like you did when you were a child. Pitching tantrums, acting a fool. People don't really grow up. They get older, sure, but there's a part of them stuck in past."

I look at Mom and Sam. She's trying to get him to dance

and he's shaking his head, no way. But they're both grinning. I wonder what they were like when they were kids.

Florence sniffles. I notice her watching Ford and the other little kids.

Missy asks, "You OK, Florence?"

"I am," she says, wiping a tear from her cheek. "Just happy, is all."

Charlotte whispers to my mom, then points to her watch. They both run down the breezeway and disappear. A few minutes later, my mom reappears alone. She grabs one of the lawn chairs and moves it onto a sidewalk. She climbs onto the chair, and stands, using Sam as a crutch to the side.

"Everyone, can I have your attention?" Mom shouts. She is waving everyone in like a circus ringleader. "Gather around. Come on, closer now. Dale, can you turn down the music? Thanks. Rex, Missy, over here. Sadie, grab your little sister please. Yes, Charlotte, you too. Come on."

"What's all this about?" Missy whispers in my ear.

I can't help but smirk. "You'll see."

"You know. Tell me!" Missy pokes, agitated. "I hate surprises."

"*Shhh*. But get ready to eat some cake."

"First, I want to thank everybody for coming. Summer is almost over, and it's always good to have one last hurrah. But while we have you, I want you to help me in celebrating someone very special to me—"

I look at my feet, my face flushing with embarrassment, but this time, it's mixed with pride.

"Birthdays only come once a year, but milestone birthdays come far less, and deserve far more attention—"

Mom looks so beautiful right now, standing on the chair, the sun rays behind her. She's looking right at me. Now I'm smiling so hard, my whole face tightens so much it almost hurts.

"And that's why I'd like you to give a round of applause to our neighbor, Florence Jones-Smith. Happy seventy-fifth birthday, Florence!"

The crowd hoots and hollers and claps. Sam whistles. Ford shouts, "Yeah, yeah, yeah!" My mom steps down to help Charlotte with the cake. It's covered in too many candles to count. The gathering parts as they walk toward me . . . no, toward Florence. Everyone is singing, *"Happy birthday to you . . . Happy birthday to you . . ."*

I feel like I've been punched in the gut. My eyes are burning, and the tightness in my face stays, but it's not the same. I'm not smiling anymore. I'm glaring daggers at my mom.

"Happy birthday, dear Florence. . . . Happy birthday to you."

The cake is less than two feet away from me. It's the sheet cake from our fridge. The box window only let me see the top part, *Happy Birthday*. Below, it says *Florence* in frosted pink cursive. Bile and hate burn my stomach, my chest, my throat.

Flashes in my mind: Slapping the cake to the ground. Throwing it at my mom. Screaming at her. Tossing over the long table with all the food. Shrieking at the top of my lungs. Running through the crowd, pushing people back. Shouting, "Fuck you!" in every single face.

But I don't do that. I don't do any of that.

I watch Florence blow out the candles.

Everyone claps.

"Who wants some cake?" my mom calls out.

When she looks at me, I can't help myself. Years of rage

roars through me, and now I'm roaring, "*I hate you. I fucking hate you!*"

I storm off. I am slamming my feet against the ground as hard as I can, as if I weigh a hundred tons. Everyone is staring, but I don't care. Years of public embarrassment from my mom has left me immune. When I pass through the gate to the pool, I lunge back and throw it as hard as I can. The metal clangs, ringing through the air like a war bell.

"R-rex, g-get b-back h-here this in-instant!"

I'm almost to the other side of the pool, to the other gate, just twenty feet from my apartment. Once I'm inside, I will scream and I will rage. I will let out the anger inside me before it burns me alive. Behind me, I hear the running footfalls before they're on me. Mom's hand lands on the back of my head, her slapping me as hard as she can. The hand comes down again, and again. As she slaps me, she screams, "*What is wrong with you?!*"

I keep moving forward. Every part of me is on fire. I want to hurt someone. I want to scream. I want to cry. I want to kick her, the way I feel kicked.

Her fingers find my hair, taking it hostage. She yanks me back so hard, I almost fall. I can see the second gate, ten feet from my door. But now I'm not walking toward it, I'm being led, dragged by my hair. My own shout is shrill, like my mother's. "*Let me go!*"

She pushes me inside, throwing me to the carpet. She yells, "What was that about?!"

"What do you think?!" I bellow back.

"I don't know! That's why I'm asking!"

For a second, I'm astonished. I can find no words. She doesn't know. She really doesn't know.

Then my rage reignites, made all the worse by the gasoline she just dumped on it.

"*It's MY fucking birthday!*" I shriek. "And you forgot! Like you always forget!"

Mom's fury drains out of her. For a second, she's dumbfounded. Like I did hit her. She stands there in the apartment, trying to think of an answer.

Mom says, quietly, "It's just another day. Who cares?"

"*I* care!"

"It's not that big a deal," Mom snaps.

"If it's not a big deal, then why did you just make a big deal out of Florence's birthday?!"

"Because Florence needs it. Did you know her children died of typhoid decades ago? Did you know her twin sister passed away the year before last? She has it rough. You don't. You're living the good life. This day should be about *her*—not about you. You have plenty of birthdays left. Plenty!" As Mom speaks she gets louder, her intensity increasing until she's screaming. "Because she's *seventy-fucking-five*! Why do you have to ruin her special day?!"

"*Because it's MY special day too!*"

I stand. I'm screaming, inches from Mom's face. So angry, everything is red. I don't know the words coming out of my mouth. My body is dry, but my swimsuit is still wet. Water trickles down my leg. Suddenly, I'm starkly aware how cold it is inside our air-conditioned apartment compared to the summer heat outdoors, as the water on my leg feels like an ice snake. But I'm still screaming.

Then Mom has my hair in her grip again, and she's dragging me into the kitchen, opening drawers, grabbing for something in the knife drawer, and I'm shouting "*What are you doing?!*" and I'm pulling to get away, but she won't let go, and I hear blades scraping against blades and then she has something in her hand, and I think this is it, she's done with me, and I'm screaming, "*Don't, please don't!!*"

Trying to escape, I fall backward, and she's on top of me, her knee on my chest, her hands launching at my face, and I see the scissors. She grabs my hair, and she snips. "*What are you doing?!*" Snips again. Snip. Snip. "*Stop it, what are you doing?!*" I put my hands up, and I feel a cut, and then a slash. And another. The scissors plunge at my face again and again. "*You're going to cut out my eyes! Stop!*" I tuck my face into the crook behind my elbow, trying to protect my eyes. I feel the scissors cut into my forearm on their way to my hair. Snip. Snip. Snip. "*Stop!!*"

"*You wanna make me look bad in front of everyone?*" she shrieks. "*Then I'll make you look bad in front of everyone!*"

The scissors come down again and again. Snip. Snip. Every ounce of me wants to fight, wants to run, but I can't. Snip. Snip. If I hurt her, I'm just like Sam. If I try to run, she could stab me in the back. Snip. Snip. So I lie there. I try to be still. Snip. To stop moving. Snip. Close my eyes. Snip. Become a statue. Snip. Pretend I'm a rock. Snip. In the game Rock, Paper, Scissors—

Snip.

—scissors can't hurt the rock—

Snip.

—so I have to be a rock.

Snip.

Snip.

Snip.

From somewhere behind, Sam shouts, "*Wh-what are y-you*

d-doing, L-l-luciana?!" He yanks Mom off of me. He tosses her to the side, into the hallway. When I open my eyes and look up at him, looking at me, I see nothing but horror in his eyes. The kitchen and my body look like a salon floor. Lengths of my hair are scattered everywhere. Along with spots of blood.

Sam drives me two towns over, to Coppell. He takes me to a Mexican barbershop, one we've never been to before. He walks me inside. The barber says, "Lo siento. We just closed." Then he sees me. His eyes grow so large, I can see the whites all the way around.

Sam says, "P-p-please?"

The old man nods.

I sit down in the chair. There's a boy in the reflection. He looks like me, but he's not. I don't recognize him. Some of his hair is the length mine was. Down to his neck, under his chin. Other parts are only two or three inches long. Some are absent, all the way to the scalp. There is no design there, no rhyme or reason. Just random peaks and valleys.

And small red cuts dotted and lined everywhere. His scalp. His forehead. His cheeks. His neck. His forearms. His hands.

He looks like me, but his eyes are hollow. Like his soul left the building.

Sam says to the barber, "J-j-just sh-shave it. Sh-shave it all off."

After, Sam claps me on the shoulder and says, "L-l-looks g-good. M-military-style. L-like wh-when I was in the army."

I say nothing.

"N-new hair, n-new attitude."

I get into his truck and put on my seat belt.

On the drive home, Sam doesn't say anything else. He stares ahead at the road. I look out the passenger window, watch the white lines on the side of the road, snaking alongside us, changing, moving. Dotted lines. Solid lines. The side of the road is all dirt and trash and rocks.

I wonder if my mutant superpower finally kicked in. I wonder if I did change to stone. Not outside, but inside. 'Cause I don't feel anything.

Not mad. Not sad. Not happy.

Nothing.

"Sh-she's n-not w-well," Sam finally says. "Y-you know that, r-right?"

"Yeah," I finally say in a raspy voice, my throat tender and scratchy from screaming earlier. "But neither am I."

questions

"You s-sure you d-don't want to come?" Sam asks. He and Ford are getting their shoes on to leave.

"Oh, I'm sure." Mom laughs. "Doris hates me."

"R-rex?"

"I'll pass," I say. I've been wanting to get Mom alone. Since Sam told me what he did. Since my haircut. Since her latest fight with Sam. It's hard to talk to her when anyone else is around.

When it's just me and her, sometimes, I get a glimpse of how she is, maybe, when she's alone. When it's just *her*.

After the door closes, I ask, "Will you come sit down with me?"

Raising an eyebrow, Mom asks, "Why?"

"I want to talk."

"About what?"

"Everything."

She sits. It's still early, but the summer sun is beaming in through the blinds. Little motes of dust float through the air like fairies. My sister sits in the pink chair, nodding. Reminding me to go slow.

I ask, "Are you OK?"

Mom laughs a hollow laugh. "What? Of course. Why? Do I seem not OK?"

"You attacked me last week. On my birthday."

"I didn't attack you," she growls, getting defensive. "We had a fight. That's what parents and teenagers do."

"I don't know of any parents who chop off their kid's hair with scissors."

"Well!" she says loudly. "You were being a brat!"

"You're right. I was," I say. "Because you forgot my birthday."

"I can't remember everything!" she yells, standing up.

"Please," I say as calmly as I can. "Sit back down. I don't want to fight."

I wait. Finally, she sits. "I don't want to fight either."

"Then why are we always fighting?"

She huffs. "I don't know. That's what people do."

"Aren't you tired?" I ask. "I'm tired."

"Of what?"

"Of this. Sam hurts you. You hurt me. I hurt . . . everyone, it feels like. And now, even with Sam not picking fights, you're doing it."

"No, I don't!"

"OK," I say.

I take a deep breath. My sister presses her lips together, squeezes her hands. I realize I'm doing the same. Sitting, both legs on the couch, Mom's shorts ride up. She tugs them down. But not before I see a bruise. A new one.

"We're stuck," I say. "We can't keep doing it. It's been ten years of this. *Ten years.*"

"It hasn't—" Mom starts, but I cut her off.

"It has."

"How do you know?"

"Because that's when Marisa died."

Mom stops. She doesn't deny it, but she looks confused.

"Do you remember Marisa? My sister? You were pregnant. You and Sam got in a fight. She died."

"I . . . I mean . . . vaguely. I don't . . . why are we talking about this?"

"Because I need to know."

"Know what?"

"That you know. That it happened. And it's horrible that it happened. But it happened, and I don't know if you've ever dealt with it. I don't know if you even remember. Because I've asked and sometimes, a lot of times, you don't. But I remember what you told me when I came back from Tennessee—and *how* you told me."

Mom stares off into the living room as if the living room isn't there. As if we're on the edge of the world, and she's staring off into the cosmos. Clouds of stardust, lit by the glow of distant suns. Her face is almost orange with the light. Her eyes alive, but not. Trying to recall something she doesn't want to.

"That was a long time ago. Why are you even thinking about it?"

"Because I think about it every day. Every. Single. Day. Not a day goes by—"

"Why?"

"Because you told me it was my fault."

"No, I didn't."

"You did."

We sit there for a while. Me thinking about how to talk about this. What to say next. She looks at me, frustrated. She watches me watch her, waiting for more. Finally she says, "What?"

I ask, "Did that break you? Or were you broken before?"

"What does that mean?"

"It means, I feel broken. I am in pain all the time. Because Sam hits me, because he hits you, because you hit me—"

"I don't—" she starts, but one look from me shuts her down.

"You do. And on my birthday, I thought, this is it. She's going to—"

"Going to what?"

"Kill me."

She stares. Then she moves forward, and I jump back.

She says, "I was going to hug you. Don't act like you're scared of me."

"I *am* scared of you."

We sit there. Taking each other in. I don't know what she sees. But what I see? This woman. Thick, but not fat. Muscled, from waiting tables. Long legs, but not too long. The bruise peeking out, the one I didn't know about until now. Her attitude is strong. Defiant. Not a dab of makeup on her tanned, olive-complected face. She uses lemon juice to make her brown hair blond. But her hair's a tangle, unwashed, uncombed. She never gets ready 'til she has to go to work at night. If I'm sixteen, that makes her . . . thirty-six.

But she looks younger. Like she's my age. She's not a mom. Not my mom. She's not even an adult. She's just some . . . teenager, trapped in a body that kept aging. Like something happened when she was young and she just . . . stopped. In the light, she looks like a mosquito trapped in amber.

Was it Marisa that made her snap? Was it her own family? Her father? Was it the snow globe that she lost in the snow? Or was it everything? Was life just too much, piling one pain on top of another until it crushed her?

Sam has stopped fighting—or I thought he had. But she hasn't. She's still ready to rumble. Even now. In her eyes, I can see her confusion at my approach. At wanting to just sit down and talk.

"You can't be scared of me," she says, her lower lip quivering. "You're my son. I love you. I would never hurt you."

The strange thing is—she means it.

She is not one thing or the other. She is not some easy answer. She is my mother—and a stranger too.

I could keep hating her.

Or I could try . . . try to love her.

No matter how it hurts.

playground

I'm sitting on the swings at the edge of the apartment complex. No one is here. Which makes it a nice place to watch the sun setting in the west.

The whole sky is on fire as the sun starts to dip behind the horizon. Like a brilliant egg of light bursting open, but in reverse.

Summer's over, and school will start up again soon. I'll see my friends and make good grades and graduate and move away. Only two more years, then I can leave, go to college . . . if I get a scholarship or some grants or find money somewhere. I don't know. I'll figure it out. But I will go away. I will leave. Start over. But just me.

Sam hasn't hit Mom lately. But he's come close. 'Cause she's hit him.

He's changed, but she hasn't. And she doesn't like that he's changed.

Sometimes I try to stop them. Sometimes I walk away.

And I feel guilty for that.

Like I'm always walking away.

Always gone at the wrong time.

Like everything is my fault.

Isn't it?

No.

My sister sits on the swing next to me. She is smiling a little, like I said something silly. *It's not your fault, you know. It was never your fault.*

"But I wasn't there. Mom said—"

She was wrong to say that. It's not your fault.

"If I had been there, I might have—"

You were a child. Seven years old. It's not your fault.

"I could have stopped it, or changed the outcome—"

No one can change the past. It's not your fault.

"But—"

Stop. No more. It wasn't your fault. It was never your fault. It will never be your fault. So let it go. Move on.

I find myself crying on the swing, watching the sun finally vanish below the edge of the world. The clouds like tentacles of red, trying to cling to the day, to hold the light a little longer, but it's too late.

"I don't like when it's dark," I say.

Marisa says, *It gets dark sometimes, big brother. But the sun always comes up tomorrow. Focus on that.*

"I'm scared."

I know. But that's OK. Everything will be OK.

"You can't say that."

I just did.

The wind blows and the swing next to me moves. For a

second, I imagine Marisa can do it, actually move the swing she sits on. She kicks her legs, and pulls her arms just-so, until she starts to gain some air, swinging back and forth. Up and down. Up and down. Laughter filling the air.

I join her.

We swing together for a long time . . .

In fact, we're still swinging.

AFTERWORD

I survived.

Repeating that is good. It's important to remind yourself—after something truly awful has happened to you—that you are still alive, that you are still kicking, that you can keep going. That you survived.

We are all survivors. We all have a past. We all have tragedy in our lives. We all have dark moments that we want to forget, or at the very least forgive. And forgiveness is important.

I do a lot of school and library visits for my first book, *Free Lunch*. Some of the questions that always come up include: *Did the violence stop? Did you ever forgive your mom? And do you still have a relationship with her?*

The short answers are *No, Yes*, and *No*.

As it does, the violence continued in my house. It came and went, but it was always present. Which is why I moved out at age sixteen and moved in with my abuela to finish high school. I got good grades and went on to graduate from the University of Texas at Austin. Then I moved to New York City and managed to earn myself several dream jobs, including editing comic books. There were a few years of self-harm, because on some level, I missed the violence. But eventually, I made a decision that I didn't want that in my life anymore. So I stopped. I have been violence-free for over a decade now. I am grateful for that.

As for forgiveness, it took a long time, but after ten years of living away from her, I did forgive my mom. I couldn't forget, but I could forgive. And carrying around all that hate and anger and sadness inside me? It didn't do anyone any good. Especially me. It was better to let go of the past, to stay in the present, and to focus on happy tomorrows. As for forgiving myself, and loving myself—that's something I am still working on. Every single day.

And for the final question, no, I don't have a true relationship with my mom. Or my stepdad. They have since split, and both have remarried to other people. And divorced again. I don't know much about their current lives, but whatever they're doing, I don't pass judgment on them. It's not my place. It doesn't serve any purpose. I don't have a relationship with them, because it wasn't healthy. And when I have tried to reconnect, I realized that—while I have changed—they have not. Or at least, not enough. As hard as it was, I chose to let go of toxic relationships and focus on positive connections. I have new friends, new family, a new partner, and a good life.

I am learning to be happy.

I am telling you all this because I want you to know (again) that I survived. And that whatever you've gone through, you've survived it to be here, in the present. Now. But if you're anything like me, you're carrying a lot of pain. My advice? Let it go. Let the past be the past. Move forward.

Yes, life can be dark. It can be pain. It can be agony. But it can also be sunshine. And birds chirping. And the song of the ocean tide rolling back and forth. It can be a child's laughter. It can be your own laughter. Life can be good too.

Life is never perfect, but is always many things—often at once.

Please, remember to try and enjoy it.

Best,
Rex Ogle

If you or someone you know is experiencing violence, depression, anxiety, or suicidal thoughts, please know that you are not alone, and there is help. There are people trained to listen without judgment and to connect you with resources or information that you need.

The services listed below are free and available 24 hours a day, 7 days a week, 365 days a year.

NATIONAL DOMESTIC VIOLENCE HOTLINE
Provides lifesaving tools and immediate support to enable victims to find safety and live lives free of abuse.
1-800-799-SAFE (7233)
www.thehotline.org

SUBSTANCE ABUSE AND MENTAL HEALTH
SERVICES ADMINISTRATION
Provides free, confidential 24/7 services for individuals or families facing mental and/or substance-use disorders.
1-800-662-HELP (4357)
www.samhsa.gov/find-help/national-helpline

NATIONAL SUICIDE PREVENTION LIFELINE
Provides 24/7 free and confidential support to people in emotional distress or suicide crisis.
1-800-273-8255
www.suicidepreventionlifeline.org